101 Smart Questions to Ask on
Your Interview

101 Smart Questions to Ask on Your Interview

4TH EDITION

By

RON FRY

CAREER
PRESS

The Career Press, Inc.
Wayne, NJ

101 SMART QUESTIONS TO ASK ON YOUR INTERVIEW, 4TH EDITION
TYPESET BY EILEEN MUNSON
COVER DESIGN BY HOWARD GROSSMAN/ 12E DESIGN
COVER PHOTO BY RAWPIXEL.COM
Printed in the U.S.A.

To order this title, please call toll-free 1-800-CAREER-1 (NJ and Canada: 201-848-0310) to order using VISA or MasterCard, or for further information on books from Career Press.

CAREER
PRESS

The Career Press, Inc.
12 Parish Drive
Wayne, NJ 07470
www.careerpress.com

Library of Congress Cataloging-in-Publication Data
Names: Fry, Ronald W., author.
Title: 101 smart questions to ask on your interview / by Ron Fry.
Other titles: One hundred and one smart questions to ask on your interview
Description: 4th edition. | Wayne, NJ : Career Press, Inc., [2016] | Includes
  bibliographical references and index.
Identifiers: LCCN 2015039059| ISBN 9781632650351 (alk. paper) | ISBN
  9781632659637 (ebook : alk. paper)
Subjects: LCSH: Employment interviewing.
Classification: LCC HF5549.5.I6 F757 2016 | DDC 650.14/4--dc23
LC record available at http://lccn.loc.gov/2015039059

Contents

INTRODUCTION

How to Be a Great Prospect

"Today's economy requires job hunters to be more proactive, more sophisticated, and more willing to go through brick walls to get what they want. Employers no longer plan your career for you. You must look after yourself, and know what you want and how to get it."

—Kate Wendleton,
Interviewing and Salary Negotiation

I included the above quote in the last edition of this book, published in 2009. So how has the job market changed? Well, according to most economists, the Great Recession that destroyed millions of jobs ended that year, in June, to be precise. I doubt that the college graduates of the last seven years noticed—most of them still faced an unwelcome and unhealthy employment environment that featured hundreds of overqualified applicants for the most menial of jobs. And their older brethren fared little better, enduring unending rounds of layoffs and consolidations. For all except the one-percent elite, wages have been virtually stagnant for the entire new century.

There has been one major development since the last edition of this book. According to the *Wall Street Journal*, hundreds of companies—including 457 of the Fortune 500—are using some form of "personality" testing that aims to correlate specific personality traits with success in a particular job. One test vendor, Infor, claims to assess more than one million candidates a month.

While tests such as Myers-Briggs and the MMPI (Minnesota Multiphasic Personality Inventory) were popular during the 1960s and '70s, we are clearly in a new age that *Time* magazine noted "is being driven by a collision of two hot trends: Big Data and analytics...The result is a mostly unchallenged belief that lots of data combined with lots of analytics can optimize pretty much anything...even people. Hence, people analytics." We are clearly headed to the Human Resources version of Match.com, with serious repercussions for future job candidates—what one pundit has called the "era of optimized hiring."

I will leave it to others to argue whether it is possible (or desirable) to accurately test for job-specific "success traits." Whatever you believe about this new trend, it is clearly another obstacle many of you will need to hurdle.

So let's get started

Most job candidates think of the interview in completely the wrong way—as an interrogation or police line-up. And they see themselves as suspects, not as the key prospects they really are.

This book will show you that you are, to a very large degree, *in charge of the interview*. It will convince you that you are there not only to sell the company on *you*, but to make sure that *you* are sold on *them*. It will give you the powerful questions that will work whatever your age, whatever your experience, whatever your goals.

It will *not*, however, spend very much time preparing you for the questions the interviewer is going to throw at *you*. Luckily for you, I've already written the companion book to this one— *101 Great Answers to the Toughest Interview Questions*—whose sole purpose is to do exactly that. And I have just revised it as well. Using these two books together, you will be amply armed for any interview and any interviewer.

Even though I think you should buy a copy of my other book, I am going to reveal a secret that may cost me sales: There really aren't 101 questions you have to prepare yourself for. Not even a dozen. There are only six:

Can you do the job?

Do you have the specific qualifications I'm seeking? Do you have the right degree? The right experience? The appropriate skills? Or, to use the current in-vogue term, the appropriate *competencies*?

Will you do the job...

better than the other people I'm interviewing? Prove to me that you're the best person for the job by giving me great answers to *my* questions and showing your interest by asking me equally detailed questions.

Will you actually *take* the job if I offer it to you?

How hungry are you? How much do you actually want *this* specific job? Or are you so desperate you'll take *any* job...even this one?

Even if you are perfectly qualified and highly motivated, do I think you will fit in with the rest of the group?

The smaller the company or department, the more important this "chemistry" question becomes. In a one- or two-person office, it may be the *key* question. Many managers base their hiring decisions on an overemphasis of candidates' qualifications, but then wind up firing them because of a misfit with the company culture.

Will you make me, the interviewer, look like a genius for recommending or hiring you?

Or will your miscues and missteps make me look like an idiot, kill my promotion, slash my bonus, maybe even jeopardize my own job? (The higher up on the food chain the interviewer is, the more central this question becomes to her.)

What are you going to cost me...

in money, time, and effort? How long before you actually start contributing to my bottom line? And what will I have to expend to get you there? Will you ever be asked these simple, specific questions? Probably not. Instead, you will be asked dozens of questions about your strengths and weaknesses, your successes and failures, your plans and ideas. Just remember: The answers to *these* five questions are what all the *other* questions are really trying to establish.

Why ask questions?

Crafting concise, targeted, enthusiastic, and positive responses to the interviewer's questions gives you an opportunity to demonstrate your knowledge of the company and industry and show how your qualifications would help you fit right in. *Asking* concise, targeted, and well-crafted questions gives you additional chances to demonstrate the extent of your research, build rapport, and align what you know and can do with what the company needs.

These questions, by their very nature, proclaim that *you are interested*. Likewise, the complete *lack* of questions will undoubtedly convince most interviewers that you are not. Oh, you *were* interested? You just didn't *have* any questions? Sorry, interviewers don't consider that an option. No questions? No job offer. That's certainly a rule with a vast majority of interviewers.

As I'm going to emphasize throughout this book, asking questions the smart way is just another way to match your skills, talents, and qualifications—your competencies—to the company's needs, another opportunity to demonstrate that you are far and away the only candidate the interviewer should consider. By preceding many of your questions with a phrase or statement that reminds the interviewer of something you said earlier or a point you want to continually reemphasize, you have another opportunity to "blow your own horn":

> *"Mr. Jones, as my stint at Eubonics, Inc., clearly shows, I have the ability to motivate a team to overachieve while staying on budget, but could you tell me a little more about the individuals I'd be working with (or supervising) here?"*

How to construct smart questions

Let me save the obsessive-compulsives among you some time—there are far more than 101 smart questions in this book. Because, there are a near-infinite number of specific, qualifying, clarifying questions you can ask once you receive an answer to a more general question. I will point you in the right direction, but the details of such questions are going to be determined by your exact situation, by what you've already said during the interview, and by what the interviewer has already said. How much (or little) research you've done will also expand (or limit) the depth and breadth of your questions.

Here's an example of how to construct dozens of great questions after asking a general question and receiving a relatively innocuous reply from the interviewer:

> You: Mr. Barton, I noticed in the latest issue of *Publisher's Weekly* that you intend to increase the number of books you publish next year from 250 to 400.

> Him: Yes, we do. (Hmmm, lot of detail there. Would it have killed him to give you *something* more to go on?)

Here are just *some* of the questions that would naturally evolve from this initial exchange:

"What led the company to make that decision?"

"Who made that decision?"

"Were you involved in that decision?"

"Do you know in what categories the additional books will be published?"

"How did you settle on 150 additional books?"

"Are you going to publish in categories other than your traditional ones?"

"Do you have a feel for the kinds of new books you're seeking?"

"How would that expansion affect my position? My department? My superior? My subordinates?"

"Is my position being created in whole or in part because of that decision?"

"Will others have to be hired as well? In what departments?"

*"I know sales of digital editions have become a
growing segment of most publishers' revenues.
Does this decision mean the company believes the
market for printed books is bouncing back?"*

*"What is the mix of the new books, in terms of fiction
versus nonfiction, hardcover versus paperback?"*

*"Are any of the new titles going to be published as
digital editions only?"*

*"Is the company able to fund this expansion
without going to the capital markets?"*

I could go on and on. And, in fact, for every answer Mr.
Barton gives to each of the above questions, *another* half
dozen questions should easily spring to mind. Follow-up questions are the heart and soul of the interview process...*from
both sides of the desk.*

While I'll be talking much more about how to phrase
follow-up questions in the chapters to come, let me point out
one thing our hypothetical candidate did in a couple of the
above questions: She *assumed the position.* In other words, she
referred to *"my* department," *"my* superiors," and *"my* position," *implying that the job was already hers.* Such a subtle strategy may have no effect if she is otherwise unqualified for the
job, but it *may* turn out to be the "tipping point" if she winds
up neck and neck with another candidate.

And, of course, many of her questions showed a good
understanding of the publishing process and the current state
of the industry.

So, do you have any questions?

In a traditionally structured interview, this question occurs
very near the end of the interview. In fact, you may well assume

that its appearance signals that end. Such an interview proceeds along the lines the interviewer has set in order for him to ascertain whether you have what it takes to move on to the next round.

If you are unsure of how much you want a particular job, there is nothing wrong with letting the interviewer take the reins and direct the conversation. Through her questioning, you will probably get a much clearer understanding of what exactly she is looking for…and whether that person is you (or whether you *want* to be that person).

But do you have to wait until the interviewer puts you through the wringer, smiles benevolently, and actually asks, "So, do you have any questions?" I really don't think so, especially if you have decided it is a job you want and are qualified for, in which case I would be more assertive and start asking my own questions. Just keep a couple of caveats in mind.

First and foremost, always ask permission to ask the first couple of questions. Once it's clear the interviewer has no problem with *your* asking questions even as she continues to pepper you with her own, you will have established some easy rapport and won't need to ask permission each time. But it's up to you to make sure the interviewer is comfortable with your approach. If he shows obvious signs of discomfort—frowning while saying okay, pursing his lips, or showing in any other way that he clearly is *not* too keen on your interrupting his supposedly well-crafted approach to the interview session—back off!

But if an interviewer suggests you are free to ask questions at any time or tells you it's fine when you ask permission, do so! In that case, waiting for the ubiquitous "Do you have any questions?" is a bad move: The interviewer may have already downgraded you because you *didn't* take her (strong) hint to be assertive right from the start.

Asking questions during the regular interview does not mean interrupting. And it doesn't mean always answering an interviewer's question with a question of your own, which may well thwart the interviewer's attempts to assess your strengths. Taking the initiative and asking questions early (with the interviewer's permission, of course) is the scenario I prefer, both as an interviewee and an interviewer.

As an interviewer, it impresses me. It makes me believe (barring evidence to the contrary) that the person in front of me is interested, engaged, and assertive.

As an interviewee, I want to exert some control of the interview—subtly steering it in the direction *I* want it to go—and asking questions early and often certainly accomplishes that. Doing so is especially effective with an inept (or at least less-than-veteran) interviewer, who may welcome your help!

Another great reason to ask questions early and often is because it transforms a stilted, traditional "Q & A"—with you being the "A"—into a *conversation*. By definition, this makes the meeting less formal, less "you vs. me," more "we." And a conversation is how you explore areas of common interest, trade comments, chat rather than "talk." In other words, the way you establish the personal chemistry that is one of the vital factors in landing any job. Once the applicant pool has been whittled down to a select two or three candidates, there is usually little difference between their qualifications. What differentiates one from another may well be the relationships established during the interview process...and the interviewers' assessments of how each candidate will fit in.

Last but not least, asking a good question is a slick way to sidestep an uncomfortable question from the interviewer (at least for the time being). How do you explain that one-year gap in your resume? Darn. You didn't want to have to talk about that failed dot-com bomb *yet*. Don't expect the topic to die. You are, at best, buying a temporary reprieve, but at least you've given yourself a little time to think about how you want to defuse a potentially uncomfortable situation.

By interspersing your own smart questions throughout the interview, when the interviewer finally asks, "Do you have any (other) questions?" to signal the end of the interview, you may well be able to reply, "No, not really, I think we've covered all the bases." And you wouldn't have to worry that she will reject you for a lack of interest…since you have clearly demonstrated your interest throughout the interview.

How to use this book

It's as important to know how and when to ask a question as it is to know what questions to ask. In chapter 1, we'll talk about questioning "strategy"—general rules to follow to ensure your questions are concise, appropriate, timely, and to the point. And that they actually accomplish what you want them to.

Chapter 2 is, in my mind, the most important in the book, even though it has nothing to do with questions to ask on your interview. Rather, it details questions to ask *yourself* before you even make a phone call, answer an ad, peruse a job board, register on a website, meet with a recruiter or post a resume. It won't do you much good to have a list of fantastic questions to ask an interviewer if you're seeking the wrong job at the wrong company in the wrong industry. Chapter 2 will ensure you take the time to analyze who you are, what's important to you, and what you ideally want in a job and a career.

Once you know where you're going, chapter 3 will give you the help you need to begin researching the companies you intend to target.

In chapter 4, you'll start constructing the smart questions to ask "pre-interviewers" employment agencies, recruiters, headhunters, and Human Resources—who can't say "yes" but can certainly say "no."

Finally in chapters 5, 6, and 7, you'll be ready to concentrate on the questions to ask the hiring manager—the person who can actually say those magic words, "You're hired! When can you start?"

Chapter 5 covers "basic" questions about the company, department, and job; "probing" questions designed to elicit more and more detail; "style" questions about your potential boss and the corporate culture; and "pre-closing" questions to get a better feel for how the interview is going and what you need to do to land the job.

In chapter 6, I give you a series of great "closing" questions—to identify hidden objections, find out about the other candidates (your competition), and push for an offer.

Finally, in chapter 7, I'll tell you what to do when you actually receive a job offer and how to get the best deal—when and how to discuss salary, bonuses, benefits, and perks and how to maximize your compensation package. I'll also discuss how to handle the rejections endemic to the job-search process.

Just remember, like playing the piano, interviewing takes practice, and practice makes perfect. My own hours of personal interviewing experience—the tragedies and the triumphs—as well as my years as an interviewer are the basis for this book. I hope to spare you many of the indignities I suffered along the way by helping you prepare for the interview of your worst nightmares at a comfortable remove from the interviewer's glare.

Enough preparation. Let's get busy.

C HAPTER 1

The Strategy of Asking Smart Questions

Before we start delving into specific questions to ask yourself, "pre-interviewers," and the hiring manager, let's agree on some overarching rules, if you will, that will govern them.

Shape your questions to the position

Learn as much as you can about the position for which you're interviewing—*before* you show up for *any* interview. When you ask questions about any aspect of the industry, company, department, or job, make sure they are couched in terms of the requirements of the specific job you're seeking and the goals of the particular company at which you hope to be hired.

Don't ask about time off

Or vacations or sick days or anything other than the job at hand...at least not before you're *offered* the job.

Don't ask about salary or benefits

Again, wait until you are offered the job. (See chapter 7 to understand why.) You don't want money to be a deciding factor when the interviewer is still wondering whether you're the best person for the job...or even worthy of a callback.

Know what to ask when of whom

Questions differ depending on both where you are in the interviewing process—screening interview, hiring interview, first, second, third, and so on—and, during a particular interview, where you are in the interviewer's script.

The earlier you are in the process, the more likely you'll be asking general questions about where the company's going, its culture, and what it deems important or valuable. Your questions are an attempt to get an initial feel for how you'd fit in, where you'd fit in, whether and how you could grow, and so on.

The more information you can get at or near the start of any interview, the easier it will be to tailor *your* answers accordingly:

Is there a written job description for this position?

What are the challenges you believe need immediate attention?

How would you describe your ideal candidate for this position?

What kinds of people seem to succeed in this company? This department? Working for you?

What particular traits do you value most in your subordinates?

What qualifications do you consider most essential to this position?

Naturally, you will continue to ask follow-up questions until the interviewer has given you a virtual "interview blueprint," effectively drawing a portrait of the candidate she wants to hire.

The more time you devote to a particular company, the more targeted and probing the questions should become, both those the interviewer will ask you and those you should ask the interviewer. You'll really want to start homing in on the particular information you need to decide whether this is the right company, position, and boss for you. So the farther along in the process, the more individualized the questions become (since what's most important to you may be something I may not ask about, like the availability of on-site daycare, reimbursement of moving expenses or tuition, and so on).

Get the interviewer talking

Ask open-ended questions-those that begin with "Who," "What," "When," "Where," or "How." Your purpose is to establish a conversation, to get the interviewer talking so he volunteers the information you want (and just maybe, to elicit some information you don't even *know* you want). These kinds of questions do that:

> **How do you see this position evolving over the next two or three years?**
>
> **What do you think is happening to book publishing as a whole? Is print dead?**
>
> **Who held this job previously? Was she promoted? What is her new title?**
>
> **When are you hoping to make your decision?**

Ask probing questions, usually open-ended, to extract more details and to follow up after general questions.

Closed-ended questions—those that can be answered by a simple yes or no (and undoubtedly will be)—are useful near the end of an interview, when you want to "close" the sale, or when you *do* want specific answers to specific questions. *"Do I have to wait 90 days for medical coverage?"* A simple yes or no will do fine.

"Why" questions can be a little tricky, since, if you're not sensitive (or aware), they can make you appear more aggressive than you might want: *I noticed you have put a lot of books out of print last year. Why did you do that?"*

You can extract the same information in a gentler way: *"It seems from your annual report that more books than usual were remaindered last year. Is that because digital editions are cannibalizing print sales?*:

Consider asking questions that *aren't* questions. Making a statement rather than asking pointed queries is a way to put a nervous interviewer at ease. It takes some practice, but it's very effective in getting reluctant interviewers to open up: *"What would help me most would be to get a better feel for the culture I'd be walking into and the styles of the people with whom I'd be working. Could you take a couple of minutes to give me a better understanding of those issues?"*

Match your style to the interviewer's

That doesn't mean you have to become a total milquetoast when interviewing with a passive interviewer, but, if facing such a scenario, you may want to appear a little less aggressive than you actually are.

That's why you have to be a little careful about a "one-size-fits-all" interview approach. Yes, employers want go-getters. Confident candidates. Enthusiastic, hard workers. But take the time to look around the office you're visiting. Is everyone pretty laidback? Then dial back your fire-breathing sales personality. You can brag about the results you achieved without scorching anybody.

Likewise, if you're inherently reluctant to blow your own horn and a little passive and laidback yourself, an Animal House–like atmosphere might not be your cup of tea.

Watch the interviewer's body language

You also need to always gauge the interviewer's response to what you're saying, not just to the answers you've given but to the questions you've asked. Listen for verbal clues and watch the body language that will often tell you how you're *really* doing. If it's obvious you've hit a wrong note, you may even want to say something like: *"I'm sorry. That question seemed to make you uncomfortable. Is that an area you're not yet prepared to talk about?"* Again, you don't want to kill a potential job offer because you were overly aggressive on the interview.

If you know what to look for, you'll get extra clues from the body language of an interviewer:

Lack of **eye contact** or "shifting" eyes are usually seen as a sign of dishonesty or, at best, discomfort: *"Mr. Interviewer, are you planning any more layoffs?"* (squint, shift, squirm, blink) *"Uh, no, Jim. So, how about dem Bears?"*

Raised eyebrows indicate disbelief or even mild distain, along the lines of: *"Oh, really?"/"You don't mean that, do you?"/"Gee, how'd you figure that out?"/"You don't actually expect me to buy that, do you?"*

A smile at the wrong time can be a sign of discomfort or an indication of a complete lack of appropriate social skills.

A tightly **clenched jaw, pursed lips** or a **forced smile** may indicate stress, anything from a boss's reprimand to an early morning fight with a spouse. While the cause is clearly not your problem, you need to make sure the effect does not become a distraction during your interview.

"Closed" positions of the hands and arms—clenched fists, arms folded across the body—are *not* positive. They may also indicate boredom or negativity.

An interviewer who is **slumping** or leaning back in his chair may be showing disrespect, arrogance or disinterest. It is surely a sign that you have to ask a question to get him back into the conversation.

If the interviewer keeps **nodding rapidly** for an extended period of time while you are asking or answering a question, it may be shorthand for, "Be quiet and let me say something now."

Doodling, chewing on a pencil, scratching, playing with her hands, moving things around on a desk, or acting distracted are typical **signs of nervousness.** Don't interpret it as anything *more* than nerves unless something else tips you off. Again, ask a question to get the focus back on you or, even better, a question about *her.* (Most people like to talk about themselves, especially a not-too-experienced interviewer who seems to be nervous about interviewing *you,* believe it or not!)

Be concise and to the point

If your question is so long and convoluted that even *you* don't remember where it started by the time you finally finish it, what do you expect the poor interviewer to think? Ask one question at a time, not a series of questions masquerading as a multi-clause construction. Then follow up with a series of equally pointed and specific questions to elicit more information.

Assume the position

Even when my brother was a relatively low-level salesperson at a public relations company, he constantly talked about what "we" were doing and how "we" were doing it and what "our" prospects were. Despite the fact that he was not privy to the executive ranks until late in his tenure—what "they" knew or where "they" were headed—his use of "we" certainly gave the impression he was more involved in those decisions than he was...and he wasn't involved at all in any of them!

It must have worked. His last title there was president of sales.

When appropriate, assume you already have the job and ask questions accordingly:

> *"Mr. Baines, what's the first challenge we're going to face together?"*

> *"Ms. Lyndon, what projections do we need to hit next year?"*

> *"Mr. Johnson, what are the three most important targets you have for my department?"*

Okay, there *are* some really dumb questions to avoid

Don't ask questions that show your lack of research:

> *"So, what exactly do you guys do?"*

> *"Who named the company?"*

> *"Do many people work here?"*

Don't ask questions that illustrate your poor sense of taste, strange sense of humor, or those that are just plain wacko:

> *"Wow, how long before I get a cool corner office like yours?"*

"So, I guess you're the Big Kahuna?"

"How many days a month can I work from home?"

"Should I tweeze my eyebrows?"

Don't ask questions that reveal your biases

"Hmm, Rutigliano, that's Italian, isn't it?"

"Will I be working with a lot of people babbling in another language?"

"Will my boss have a problem following my directions? After all, I did graduate from MIT."

Avoid questions that make it clear you are desperate:

"I really need to pay the rent by next Friday. If you offer me this job, could I get a loan before I start?"

"I've been out of work for months. What the heck do I have to do to get a job?"

"Will you please hire me? I'm willing to do anything."

And don't let your arrogance show: *"I have a few problems with the offer. Since you can't seem to do anything about it, may I talk to someone with the authority to give me what I want?"* Want to bet that offer just evaporated?

As a book publisher, I have a lot of experience with literary agents who suddenly receive a better offer for a book…right after I've made mine. Real or fictitious, such timely offers may be seen by some as just part of the negotiating process, but can also be off-putting and even deal-killing. So be careful of using a competitor's offer, be it real or imagined, in a way that can be perceived as threatening: *"Well, I appreciate the offer, but SBC Company already offered me $5,000 more. Beat it or else."* Be especially careful if you haven't really gotten any such counter-offer...even competitors talk!

It's okay to ask an interviewer about his own experience with the company—*"What do you like most about working here?" "What do you find most satisfying about your job?" "What challenges are you facing in your own position right now?"* But avoid any that are clearly too personal: *"How much did you make last year?" "Aren't you awfully young to be a vice president?" "Why isn't your office bigger?"* These would include the kind of illegal questions that you know he can't ask of you: *"Are you married?" "Tell me about your children." "Were you born in this country?" "What kind of a foreign accent is that?"*

And avoid any question that has nothing whatsoever to do with the job, department, or company. These may include, but are not limited to, asking for a date, inquiring about the "smoking break" policy, or asking any question that would lead even the most understanding interviewer to immediately call security and have you forcefully ejected, preferably from the state.

Don't introduce negativity into an interviewer's mind

There is nothing inherently wrong with asking about normal work hours, as long as you don't say, *"My last boss expected me to work most Saturdays. You don't, do you?"* Oh, yeah, you are *so* committed.

The way some questions are posed may make them negative: *"Do you have a lot of people who job-share?" "I wouldn't have to move during the next two or three years, would I?" "I'd love to work from home a couple of days a week. Any problem with that?"* It's quite possible that the company is highly amenable to job-sharing and telecommuting and has no plans to relocate anyone in your department, but equally possible that you just talked your way out of the job.

As I've noted, some questions are inappropriate just because you asked them at the wrong time. When you have been offered a job, it is expected that you will want to know all about your compensation, vacation schedules, holidays, and similar practical details. But asking how soon you can schedule a vacation during the first five minutes of an interview is not recommended.

Don't tell a joke...

...even if you and your friends think you should be the new cast member of SNL.

Most of us think we're a lot funnier than we are, and humor is—to murder a metaphor—in the ear of the beholder. Why take a chance that some lame joke costs you a job? Be at ease, feel free to smile and even offer a humorous (or at least less than serious) comment if it seems in keeping with the rest of the conversation, but please remember that you are there to convince *them* to hire you and assess whether *you* want to work there, *not* to audition for a gig at the Laff Factory.

Never let them see you sweat

It bears repeating: Don't ask questions that make you appear desperate...even if you've been terminated from your previous job!

I noticed something truly bizarre during my dating days. When I was young and single and HUNGRY, I seemed to give off vibes that screamed, *"Warning! Warning! Women beware. Desperate bachelor on the prowl."* Not long after I got married, I was out with friends and seemed to suddenly be a rock star. A surprising number of attractive women in the bar seemed interested in me.

What the heck was happening? I was never a lady killer, and my (okay, not great) looks hadn't suddenly changed. Well, my totally unscientific, unsupported premise is that the same "vibes" that had cried desperation were now sending out soothing, happy, content signals...and people were responding the way you would expect them to.

Interviewers, whether men or women, will react in the same way. Be desperate, think desperate, and you might as well walk in carrying a sign saying, "Will work for anyone, do anything, require nothing." That is not the message employers want to hear and, I suspect, not the one you want to be sending them.

This is also a factor when you are trying to find a job, *any* job, and are clearly overqualified for the ones you're pursuing. It's hard to feign interest in a job you don't really care about. Did you pick a "safety" college when you were a high school senior, one you figured you'd have no problem getting into if the places you *really* wanted to go turned you down? Did any of you get *rejected* by your safety school? Maybe when you interviewed there, you unconsciously alerted them that they *were* your "safety" school! No employer wants to hire someone who considers their company a last-ditch option.

Remember it's a two-way street

It's impossible to lead you by the hand through a whole series of potential questions—smart or not—for the simple reason that the specific questions you choose to ask should be an attempt to redefine the job so it more closely fits your qualifications. Let me explain.

In very large companies, job titles and descriptions seem to be etched in stone. But the smaller the company, the more likely there are a plethora of possible duties, not all of which any single person can do. Or not all of which any single person is qualified to do. So, especially at the smaller company (but even at many of the larger ones), you want to attempt to customize the job the employer *thinks* he is offering you so it more closely matches the qualifications you have.

Let me give you an example of how this can work. My publishing company, Career Press, has a number of editors. Two are exclusively acquisitions, meaning they find the books that the company is going to publish each season (or, at least, develop a solid list from which to choose). The others are involved in the various aspects of production, everything from working with authors on their manuscripts in a general way—move this chapter, kill that example, add a checklist—to detailed line editing, proofreading, designing the interior "look," executing that format, then getting the book off to the printer and our e-book partners.

Not long ago, we needed to hire a new editor. My editor-in-chief wanted another "word" person who could do initial editing on every manuscript that came in, then pass them off to an editor who would work with each author on the more detailed, line-by-line edits.

But then Jinny walked in and declared, *"I'm not really the kind of editor you said you were looking for. But I am the best darn formatter you ever saw. Instead of hiring a general editor, why don't you let the rest of the editors spend more time editing and I'll spend all my time designing their books, laying them out, and getting them off to the printer? And I'll design them in a way to maximize their digital impact without having to completely redesign them."*

If this happened anywhere else, especially a "big" publishing house like Random House or Simon & Schuster, the editor-in-chief probably would have said, *"Thanks, but we need someone who does this, and this only."* At Career Press, Jinny completely convinced us to change the entire structure of the editorial department.

She was not *remotely* qualified for the opening as it was described and advertised, but gave herself a chance to actually get a job by getting the company to *redefine the job so it fit her qualifications.*

She is still a great employee...who recently convinced us to let her telecommute four days a week. Some things never change!

It's okay to be a copycat

Feel free to "copy" typical interview questions *you* should expect to be asked and ask them of the interviewer instead:

What are the company's (department's) strengths and weaknesses?

What was the last great challenge faced by the department? How did you and your team handle it?

Can you tell me about a successful project and how you managed it?

Can you tell me about some recent problems you've faced and how you (as a team) overcame them?

What's your definition of success? What's your definition of failure?

If you could change one thing about the way this department works (or is structured or is managed or is compensated), what would it be?

How often do you and your team go out to socialize outside of work? Is such extracurricular activity actively promoted? Tolerated? Discouraged?

Ask for the job if you want it

The more sales-oriented the job—the more "Type A" the interviewer or the observed company culture—the more aggressively you need to close the sale. In fact, lack of real aggression in these situations will probably be reason enough to dismiss you as a viable candidate.

I think you should always try to make a selling point while asking a question, but in this case, it's virtually an imperative: *"I tried to make my cover letter and resume memorable. I'm glad you appreciated their creativity. Will that same 'out of the box' thinking be appreciated in this position?"*

Interview killers

I'm going to assume that you have already been on enough interviews (or, if you're a recent graduate, read enough interviewing books), to know that there are rules to follow during interviews. So I'm not going to discuss most of them here.

But there is a list of "no-no's" that are so important, failing to avoid them can virtually doom *any* chance you have of securing the job before the interview even starts. Given their seriousness, I thought it prudent to remind you of them.

For many interviewers, your **showing up late** is immediate cause for canceling the interview. It doesn't matter that traffic backed up, your cat threw up a hairball, or you just got lost in the elevator.

Being on time is not racing down the final corridor with moments to spare. Some interviewers agree with New York Giants football coach Tom Coughlin, who declared that team members were late for meetings if they didn't show up fifteen minutes *early*.

Poor grooming is a basic turnoff. Wearing so much perfume or cologne that a gasping interviewer lunges for the window isn't recommended. Nor is wearing more makeup than a runway model, clanking along with a pocketful of change or an armload of bangles and bells, or sporting an unkempt beard (or, for some interviewers, even fashionable stubble).

Given the tube tops, sneakers, short skirts, and patterned stockings I've seen waltz through my door (and all on one candidate!), some of you may need to review the appropriate dress for every interview.

While women no longer need to sport a black business suit and pearls, dressing tastefully in professional apparel is still a must. And that black suit will still work in most environments.

Men should wear a white or light blue shirt, conservative suit, silk tie, shined dress shoes.

No one should think of wearing ties that glow in the dark, T-shirts advertising anything (but especially not X-rated), or any clothes deemed "relaxed and comfortable" (unless you are relaxed and comfortable in a double-breasted suit).

In case you haven't gotten the message (where have you been?), **smoking** is no longer acceptable behavior…anywhere, anytime. And don't kid yourself. Just because you don't light up during an interview doesn't mean that everyone in the room isn't acutely aware that you are a smoker.

Of course, if you decide to smoke during the interview itself—and some candidates have in my office—you can go down to that front door right away to finish up.

Do not smoke even if the interviewer lights up and encourages you to do likewise.

There should be a new reality tv series featuring the **bizarre behavior** of some interviewees, as they chew, burp, scratch, swear, cry, laugh, and scream their way into our hearts. Interviewees have shown up drunk or stoned, brought their mothers with them, fallen asleep, even gone to the bathroom and never returned.

Keeping your cell phone on during the interview qualifies as inappropriate behavior. Actually receiving or making a call ranks as bizarre.

Remember what the interviewer is thinking: If this is your *best* behavior, what (*gasp!*) do I have to look forward to?

If you **lie about anything**—especially where and when you worked, what you did, where and when (or even if) you attended college—you will be caught. No matter how lowly the job, there are significant expenses involved with hiring someone to perform it. So companies will take the time to check out references. And the higher up the food chain you climb, the more intensive their scrutiny.

Even if the lie is inconsequential, the very fact that you lied will, in virtually all instances, be immediate grounds for dismissal. Lacking a particular skill or experience may not automatically exclude you from getting the job. Lying about it will. Just ask former NBC news anchor Brian Williams about the consequences of "shading" the truth or "misremembering" an experience.

While honesty may be the best (and only) policy, it is **not necessary to share anything and everything** with your interviewer. He is not your priest, and you are not in a church confessional. Anything you do in the privacy of your own home is not something you need to share.

And do be smart enough, when asked what interests you about the job, not to answer, *"Heck, I just need a job with benefits. I'm three months along and can't wait until my maternity leave starts."*

Don't underestimate the effect of your own body language on the interviewer. While many people don't mean what they say or say what they mean, their nonverbal actions reveal *exactly* what they're feeling. According to studies, *more than half* of what we are trying to communicate is being received nonverbally.

To many interviewers, your **failure to "look them in the eye"** indicates you have something to hide. So does being overly fidgety or nervous. Greet the interviewer with a firm handshake, face him or her, sit straight up, and, of course, look 'em in the eye. *Breaking* eye contact occasionally is also a good idea. Staring at someone without pause for more than a few seconds will make them nervous.

Likewise, interviewers are looking for people who are **enthusiastic** about what they do, so sighing, looking out the window, or checking your watch during a question is not creating the right impression. If you don't seem interested in the job, why should they be interested in hiring you?

A candidate once said to me, barely five minutes into our interview, *"I've got three other offers right now. What can you do for me?"*

I showed him where the exit was.

Yes, you need to be confident, enthusiastic, and cheerful (and brave and clean and reverent...), but there can be, as this example clearly illustrates, too much of a good thing.

The interviewer asks what she thinks is a simple question and you act as if she has accused you of a crime. You start to sweat, hem and haw, and try to change the subject.

What are you hiding? That's what the interviewer will be wondering. And if you aren't actually hiding anything, why are you acting so defensively?

Interviewing over lunch is a situation fraught with potential dangers. Slurping spaghetti or soup or wiping barbeque sauce off your tie is simply not attractive, even if *you* are. Ordering the most (or least) expensive item on the menu sends an unwelcome message. And what happens when the French dish you didn't understand but ordered anyway turns out to be sauteed brains?

If you can't avoid a lunch interview (and I would certainly try), use your common sense. Order something light and reasonably priced—you're not *really* there for the food, are you? Remember what Mom told you—keep your elbows off the table, don't talk with your mouth full, and put your napkin on your lap. Don't drink alcohol (even wine), don't smoke (even if your host does), don't complain about the food (even if it was lousy), and don't forget that this is still an interview!

Although many interviewers will not consider inappropriate dress, poor grooming, or too much candor as automatic reasons for dismissal in and of themselves, an accumulation of two or more such actions may force even the most empathetic to question your suitability. Some behaviors, such as dishonesty, may well lead to an immediate and heartfelt, *"Thank you…please* do not *stay in touch."*

Is it okay to take notes?

Since it's okay for the interviewer to take notes, I believe it is okay for the interviewee, too. Not just fine, but encouraged.

Why? There are a few good reasons:

You can't possibly remember everything…no matter how good your memory. And yet you certainly want to remember what *you* said, what *he* said, what seemed *right*, what felt *wrong*, titles, numbers…all the myriad things that went on during the interview. As long as you ask permission first, I believe taking notes is an absolute requirement.

Second, it is essential for your follow-up. I encourage you to write brief individual notes or emails to *every* person you meet on an interview, from the receptionist to the person who got your coffee, and even more targeted and longer letters or emails to all the people with whom you actually interviewed. How can you be sure of the correct spelling of that many names, titles, and so on without good notes? How can you make sure to answer (again) the objection you know may be the key thing obstructing your hiring? How can you schmooze the colleague who seemed a little cold to your candidacy, perhaps jealous because *he* wanted (or expected) the job?

Third, you may need to use your notes in the interview itself—jotting down a question you don't want to forget (while the interviewer drones on), a point you want to raise, an example you want to emphasize. This will allow you to bring up a point when it's the right time, which may be quite awhile down the road, even at the very end of the interview.

You should *walk in* with notes—the questions you intend to ask, specific points you want to remember, research data you want to incorporate in an answer or question. Getting the interviewer used to your "consulting my notes" makes it a lot easier to ask permission to take notes during the interview itself. But be careful. You don't want to appear to be constantly "referring to my notes" every time the interviewer asks a question: *"Where did you go to college, Jim?" "Uh, just a minute, let me consult my notes."*

Personally, I wouldn't want anything but an attractive notebook that is extracted from an equally professional looking attaché case, along with a quality pen (not a disposable). Most recent graduates might be more comfortable toting an iPad or small tablet, which I think most interviewers would now find acceptable.

I believe many if not most interviewers will interpret your note taking as a sign of professionalism and seriousness, as long as you don't keep your nose buried in your notebook or iPad the entire time.

Whatever you use, remember, the point of the interview is to listen, then talk. Write as little as you need. And if you aren't very good at note taking and listening at the same time (or taking notes while retaining eye contact), practice. No one wants to talk to your forehead.

Don't run away...yet

We've all been there—an interview that is obviously not working. Maybe it's the interviewer, maybe it's you, maybe it's the weather, maybe it's a cruel joke by the universe. In any event, the interview is clearly not going well and you are sorely tempted to get up, thank the interviewer, and run, not walk, to the safety of your bedroom.

Fight the impulse to flee. Excuse yourself, perhaps for a bathroom break. (Hey, I know it's not usually done, but right now we're trying to salvage an interview that's going down in flames.) Compose yourself. Give yourself a pep talk. Then go back in there and sell yourself.

You may actually be completely wrong for the job, which is why the interview is not going well. But that doesn't mean there aren't other jobs at that company or jobs at other companies the interviewer knows. Make the sale. You may not know the product yet, but you may get a surprise.

And if you are rejected despite your best efforts, you may learn something—especially if you ask—that will improve your interviewing skills or performance.

Should you reject an actual offer out of hand because you've decided the job, company, or boss is completely wrong? I wouldn't. Take at least a night to think about any offer away from the stresses of the interview process. Your thinking may change.

CHAPTER 2

Questions to Ask Yourself

Who are you?

What are your strengths?

What is important to you?

What specific things do you require in the job you're seeking—adventure, glamour, a bigger office, more money?

Where do you want to work? Managing how many people?

At what sized company?

With how many people under you?

What are your long-term goals?

What are your short-term goals?

What have you already done to accomplish the latter? What do you still need to do?

Whew! And you were afraid the *interviewer* was going to ask tough questions!

There are a lot of questions to ask *yourself* long before you post a resume or research a company.

Answering these questions should enable you to define both short- and long-term goals—personal, professional, and financial—and could even help you develop a roadmap to reach those dreams. Additionally, they will help you assess the fit between a company's culture, the job, the boss...and *you*. Unless you do this kind of analysis, on what basis will you evaluate job offers? As the old saying goes, if you don't know where you're going, any road will take you there.

So lets do a few lists to help you assess who you are, what's important to you, and what this analysis should tell you about the kind of company you want to work for. You'll quickly see that this is a far more detailed and completely different "assessment" than you were advised to do when collecting data for your resume.

Questions about you as a person

What are your key values?

What kinds of people do you enjoy spending time with?

Describe your personality.

What activities do you most like doing?

What activities do you least like doing?

Are you a risk-taker or risk averse?

What in your personal life causes you the most stress (relationships, money, time constraints, and so on)?

What in your personal life gives you the most pleasure?

If you had to spend 40 hours a week doing a single activity, what would it be?

What were your favorite subjects in school? Would they still be your favorites today?

What were your strongest subjects?

What games and sports do you enjoy? What does the way you play them say about you?

Are you overly competitive? Do you give up too easily?

Are you a good loser or a bad winner?

Do you rise to a challenge or avoid conflict?

What kinds of friends do you tend to have? Do you look for people who are just like you or laugh at all of your jokes?

What has caused you to break up friendships? What does this say about you?

If you were to ask a group of friends and acquaintances to describe you, what adjectives would *they* use? Why do you think they would describe you in those terms? Are there specific behaviors, skills, achievements, or failures that would cause them to choose those adjectives? What are they?

Questions about you as a professional

What kinds of people do you like working with? What kinds do you dislike working with?

What are your goals and aspirations?

What would it take to transform yourself into someone who's passionate about every workday?

What *are* your passions?

How can you make yourself more marketable in today's competitive job market?

What are your major professional accomplishments? What competencies are your strongest calling cards?

What are your most notable failures? What did you learn from each?

What would your last boss say about your work ethic? What would your coworkers say about you? Your subordinates?

List your current strengths, abilities, and values

The following list of descriptive characteristics should help you further define who you are, both professionally and personally. Circle those words or phrases that you believe describe you, and keep them in mind when assessing any job offer or any company and its attendant culture.

Active

Active in sports

Active reader

Active volunteer

Adaptable

Adventurous

Ambitious

Artistic

Attractive

Brave/heroic

Calm

Communicative

Computer literate

Confident

Courteous

Creative

Decisive

Dedicated

Detail-oriented

Directed

Dynamic

Economical

Efficient

Empathetic

Ethical

Excellent analytical skills

Excellent math skills

Experienced

Extrovert

Flexible

Fluent in other languages

Focused

Goal-oriented

Good delegating skills

Good leadership skills

Good listening skills

Good mathematical skills

Good negotiating skills

Good presentation skills

Good public speaking skills

Good sense of humor

Good team-building skills

Good time management skills

Good under pressure

Good written communicator

Graceful	Perfectionist
Handle stress well	Performer
Hard-working	Physically strong
High energy	Precise
Highly educated (level?)	Professional
Honest	Quick-thinking
Introverted	React well to authority
Learn from mistakes	Religious
Left-brained	Responsible
Like people	Right-brained
Like to travel	Risk averse
Logical	Risk taker
Love animals	Sales personality
Love children	Self-motivated
Loyal	Sports fan
Make friends easily	Strong-willed
Moral	Supportive of others
Musical	Tenacious
Neat	Welcome change
Obsessive	Well-groomed
Organized	(Other) _____
Passionate	_____
Passive	_____
Patient	_____

These are all positive attributes, of one kind or another, to one company or another. After you've circled all of those you believe best describe you, ask your friends if they agree with your assessment—we aren't always the best judges of our own characters, are we?

You can use this list in a few important ways. First, it will help you better answer two key questions:

How do these positives match up with the qualities you believe are necessary for success in the job/career path you've chosen?

Do you have the qualities generally associated with the level of responsibility/job title you are seeking?

Let's say you are seeking a promotion to vice president at a major corporation, which would mean significant financial responsibility and hundreds of employees under your benevolent control. You will have a problem getting an interview, let alone the job, if you can't demonstrate managerial, team-building, motivational, and financial skills and experience (among others). So if you lack all or most of those characteristics, your current goal isn't realistic, and you should instead create a plan to attain the skills and experience you need to reach your professional goals.

Another important question is suggested by this list:

How many of these qualities/abilities do you *want* to use in your job?

Alternately, how many of the qualities you've deemed most important to your sense of self do you *need* to involve in your job? Only you can figure this out, but I suspect most people would be happy if their jobs utilized *more* of their abilities and interests rather than fewer. I dare say the happiest people I've ever met are those able to employ the qualities, skills, and talents they deem important at a company at which *those specific attributes* lead to success.

Another way to utilize this list is to identify qualities you believe are important to your next job or your future career but that you lack. This will enable you to create a plan to develop, attain, or obtain what you want and need to succeed in your chosen path and reach your expressed goals.

What kind of life are you seeking?

How can you know what you want if you haven't taken the time to assess what's really important to you? Look at the list of values on page 47 (adapted from the book *Targeting the Job You Want*, one of an excellent series produced by the Five O'Clock Club, a top job-search group). Rate how important each is to you—"1" for least important, "4" for most:

Of those descriptions marked "4," identify the five *most* important to you right now. Then, of *those* five, admit which you would give up (if any) if you had to. Which would you *never* give up, no matter what?

1.	
2.	
3.	
4.	
5.	

Based on this exercise, you should be able to compose a brief paragraph describing the values of the company you'd (ideally) want to work for and the job you'd (ideally) love to have.

___Adventure

___Being considered an expert

___Challenging tasks

___Chance to advance

___Chance to create

___Chance to grow

___Chance to have an impact

___Chance to lead

___Chance to learn

___Chance to participate

___Clear expectations

___Clear procedures

___Competition

___Creativity

___Enjoyable colleagues

___Enjoyable surroundings

___Enjoyable tasks

___Excitement

___Fast pace

___Freedom from worry

___Glamour

___Having responsibility

___Helping people

___Helping society

___Independence

___Influencing people

___Intellectual stimulation

___Leadership

___Meeting challenges

___Money

___Moral fulfillment

___Personal growth

___Power

___Prestige

___Public contact

___Recognition from peers

___Recognition from society

___Recognition from superiors

___Slow pace

___Stability (security)

___Structure

___Time with family

___Working alone

___Working for something you believe in

___Working on a team

The practical aspects of your job hunt

In addition to the kind of person you are, which will give you a better idea of the kind of people you want to work with and the environment in which you want to work, there are some more mundane questions you need to ask yourself:

Where (geographically) do I want to work?

Do I prefer a large city, small city, town, or somewhere as far away from civilization as possible?

Do I prefer to live and work in a warm or cold climate?

At what size company do I want to work? (Define your terms—by sales, income, employees, etc.)

What kinds of products/services/accounts would I prefer to work with?

Do I mind traveling frequently? What percentage of my time would I consider "reasonable"?

How much time am I willing to devote to a daily commute? At what point will its duration impact my other priorities (family, hobbies, etc.)?

What salary would I like to receive?

What's the *lowest* salary I'll accept?

What benefits, such as an expense account, medical and/or dental insurance, company car, and so on, do I require?

Is a tuition reimbursement plan important to me?

Is it important that the company have a formal employee training program?

Am I willing to sign a restrictive covenant, such as a noncompete clause?

Am I willing to assign copyrights or patents from my work to my employer?

If the last two questions are pertinent to your situation, I would recommend you consult an attorney before accepting that job offer. While many noncompete clauses or agreements may wind up being unenforceable, you never want to sign away anything—to work where and when you want, to retain ownership of your own ideas—without understanding exactly what you are doing.

What can you learn from past jobs and bosses?

For each job you've held in the past, describe those factors that made one enjoyable, satisfying, or rewarding and another boring, frustrating, or just plain hell. Be as specific as possible. Consider everything from the company's location, the size of its (or your) offices, perks (or lack thereof), your subordinates and supervisors, responsibilities (or lack thereof), promotional opportunities, and hours.

The more comprehensive you make this analysis, the more easily you will begin to notice behavioral patterns. This exercise may help you home in on a particular requirement (a private office), something to avoid at all costs (a boss who's passive-aggressive), or even some aspect of your own personality that you need to work on (lamenting a lack of promotional opportunities when you've never stayed at any job longer than six months!).

What can I learn from past bosses?

**How well do I interact with authority figures—
bosses, teachers, parents?**

Even if every other aspect of a job is wonderful, you could be dying to move on just because you hate your boss. Hey, it happens. But before you extract yourself from the frying pan and deposit yourself directly into the flames, you might want to do the following exercise: Make a list of every boss you've ever had, using the broadest possible definition of "boss." Divide that list into three: those with whom you *never* had a problem, those with whom you had *some* problems, and those with whom you *always* seemed to have problems.

After you've developed these three lists, try to identify the common factors that would explain the problems you had with the third group. Were they all old married white men who smoked cigars? Were they all fast-charging sales types? Were they all bosses for the same kinds of companies (large, small, whatever)?

You get the idea. The more you know about the kinds of bosses under whom you've thrived and those beneath whom you've withered, the better chance you have of finding the right fit the next time around.

I'll use myself (again) as an example. One of my early jobs in magazine publishing was as an advertising sales representative for a trade magazine. I was ambitious, passionate, and a very good salesperson. After teaching me about the basics of ad sales, my boss pretty much kept out of the way and let me run. Boy, did I run! I set a single-year sales record that, I've been told, still stands.

Now, I didn't exactly do everything by the book. In fact, I threw the book away. I ignored *all* requests to do memos or reports or anything that would have taken time away from making sales (i.e., making more money). I did not communicate, I did not summarize, I did not report. I just sold. After a short time, my boss simply stopped asking for that stuff and decided to revel in the big jump his own income was taking due to my unbridled efforts.

I did so well I got promoted to a bigger magazine, becoming the youngest sales manager in that company's history. My old boss went to my new boss and sang my praises. But he also told her to just *"let him the heck alone. He's a maverick and won't follow any of your rules. He will make you a fortune, but he doesn't want to do anything that limits his selling. Just let him sell and motivate his salespeople to sell."*

Well, my new boss wasn't nearly as flexible as my old one had been (nor, obviously, as bright). Instead of taking the recommended "hands-off" approach, she wasted days of my time in a series of meetings explaining "how we do things at *this* magazine." It was a disaster from the start, and it wasn't long before it was made pretty clear (by the vice president of sales) that one of us was not going to be left standing.

A tremendous opportunity to move up to publisher of a major consumer travel publication materialized, as if on command. It represented a huge jump in responsibility and an equally huge jump in money. The only downside was that if I wanted the job, I would have to move to the Midwest, though my wife and I were confirmed New Yorkers. Plus, she had a job she loved and informed me in no uncertain terms that she didn't intend to sacrifice her career for mine. If my new boss had simply followed my first boss's advice, I probably would have turned the job down and continued on my well-planned rise at that trade publisher.

Well, she didn't. So I had little choice. Luckily, my wife's boss found a way for her to keep her job...and do it from the Midwest. So we moved. While the situation looked fantastic, it turned out to be a company in well-hidden trouble with *two* control-freak bosses (a husband and wife, no less). I reported to both. Within ten months, I was looking for a job again...and making the move back to the New York area...where no one wanted to give me a job approaching the money or responsibility I had just had!

The result was a company called Career Press, which I founded not long thereafter, using my severance check from the Midwest. More than three decades later, it is a well-known nonfiction publisher.

Now, I am not at all unhappy that things worked out the way they did. I became my own boss, and have absolutely never regretted the unexpected path my career took. But it wasn't exactly a free choice, was it? It started with a *promotion*, of all things. Did I ask *anything* about that new boss? How compatible we were? Her style of management? Did I talk to anyone else that had worked for her? Did I talk to my predecessor in that position?

NO.

Did I ask about the salary and bonuses and special deals? You bet I did.

It gets worse. Because I was in an untenable situation, the Midwest job looked like a godsend. Well, did I ask *anything* about my two new bosses before starting to pack? How compatible were we? Their (absolutely contradictory) styles of management? Did I talk to anyone else that had worked for them? Did I talk to my predecessor in that position?

You know the answers, right?

I do not handle authority well, a surprise, I'm sure. And I guess I knew that in my heart. But I never took the time to analyze myself enough to discover how essential a part of my nature it really was. Even after it caused one meltdown, I walked right into a second.

A single aspect of *your* personality can have a similar effect on your relationship with a boss or company. Take the time to know yourself well enough to at least anticipate a problem!

Don't wear a T-shirt at a rep-tie company

Birds of a feather *do* flock together. And different companies tend to attract particular "species" of employees. A company's physical environment, management attitude and policies and the personality of the "birds" that predominate comprise its corporate culture. Is it a "loose" atmosphere with jean-clad creative types running amok? Or a buttoned-down, blue-suited autocracy with a long list of rules to follow during timed coffee breaks?

Some companies are dominated by a single personality-a still-active founder or an executive who has exerted a strong, long-lasting influence on policies and style. Think Steve Jobs at Apple, Bill Gates at Microsoft or Larry Ellison at Oracle. While there are exceptions, such companies tend to be "closely held" fiefdoms whose every level reflects the "cult of personality." If that personality is a despot, benign or otherwise, even a decentralized management structure won't create a company everyone wants to work for.

Family-owned companies often pose similar problems. Your chances to make decisions and take responsibility may be tied to your last name. Barely competent family members may wind up with cushy jobs and high pay, while you and other "outsiders" do all the work. While many such firms are privately held, even publicly traded companies in which family members hold a significant block of stock (like Ford, Walton or DuPont) may sometimes err on the side of nepotism.

Many larger, more decentralized companies will spread decision-making power and opportunities for advancement somewhat more evenly. However, such companies often encourage competition among workers rather than focusing their collective energies on competing organizations.

If managers regularly spend half their time politicking or writing self-serving memos to the boss, it's a survival-of-the-fittest (or survival-of-the-best-memo-writer) atmosphere. People attuned to corporate infighting might relish such a company; those who just want to do their jobs and be rewarded for the work they do will find it an unfriendly place to work.

Some companies are bursting with energy; their offices reverberate with a steady hum of activity. Such a high-key environment is right for aggressive go-getters who are unafraid of such a fast pace and more than ready, even eager, to jump into the fray. Other workplaces are calmer, quiet, almost studious in nature. Such low-key firms are probably better choices for those of you with more laidback personalities.

While a high-energy or low-key atmosphere says little about a particular company's chances for success, it may have a lot to do with your own on-the-job performance, success, and happiness. Matching dissimilar corporate and individual personalities usually results in a new job search.

If you run across a company that seems to give off no signals at all, beware! This is usually the directionless organization, one that lacks both an agenda and dynamic leadership. Without such leadership, you can be certain that this organization will founder, usually when things start going wrong and the timely implementation of company-wide decisions is required.

Clearly, the more you know about the companies you're considering, the better off you'll be. For those of you—and that should be *all* of you—who want to research a specific company and/or job description, Chapter 3 will give you the necessary hints and resources.

Once you've analyzed yourself and investigated a targeted company's culture, a simple but extremely important question should come to mind:

How does your self-description match that of the culture at the company you're thinking of joining?

If you are laidback and not particularly driven to over-achieve, a company that describes itself as "hard-charging" may not be for you, even if you can actually convince them to hire you.

The Gallup Organization is a unique example of corporate culture. When my good friend Tony Rutigliano was recruited by them, their offer was so enticing that it seemed like a no-brainer...until Tony asked about exactly what he'd be doing, his job title, and to whom he'd be reporting.

"Well," the recruiter confided, *"we work a little differently here. We expect that you'll wander around for a while, maybe a few months, and then you'll tell us what you really want to do. We don't really have formal job descriptions. And you can use any reasonable title."*

Needless to say, Tony, a veteran of a number of traditional magazine publishing companies, was a bit taken aback. Wander around? Create his own job description?

Since Tony was a bit of an entrepreneur at heart and a confident bloke to boot, he decided to give it a try. Luckily for him, Gallup's corporate culture, as unusual as it was, turned out to be a great fit for him.

Would it have been an equally rewarding and ultimately successful move for you? Not if you were someone who expected or required a rigid organizational chart. Anyone too uncomfortable to just "wander around" would probably have run for the hills after a couple of days (presuming they were crazy enough to take the job in the first place).

There may be nothing inherently wrong with an organization you're considering—it just might be a horrible fit *for you* and throw you completely off the career track you have outlined. Maybe you will survive, maybe you will thrive, maybe you will find yourself looking for another job in six months, maybe it will cause you to positively change your goals. In any event, you must know what you're getting into and do everything you can to prepare for that environment.

The importance of goals

I've mentioned the importance of goals already. Now it's time to emphasize them. Short- and long-term goal setting must become a habit. Once a year, reevaluate not just the progress you're making toward your long-term goals, but whether they need to be tweaked, heavily modified, or even changed completely. Life is not static. Neither are your goals—they will (and should) change with circumstance, age, position, etc.

Remember that setting goals will not only help you define where you want to go, but what you need to know and do to get there. If you have decided that you eventually want to be chief financial officer of a large corporation, you may well need an MBA or similar graduate degree. When do you plan to get it? Full or part time? If the latter, will the company allow a modified schedule so you can go to school while you work? Is there a tuition reimbursement plan? Is there already a program in place to which you can apply? Your goals and your estimation of what you need to do and be to reach them will greatly influence the questions you ask.

It's equally important to make your goals realistic. There is nothing wrong with reaching for the stars, providing you have the right size stepstool. If you aren't a high school graduate, you *can* aspire to becoming chairman of IBM, but your short-term goals better include some serious additional education! If you want to be a prize-winning author, passing a creative writing class might be a nice first step. Goals are realistic if there is a clear-cut path that you can follow to reach them. It may be a hard and long road, but if you truly believe you can actually reach its end with sufficient effort, then the goal is realistic.

Even if a goal is completely *un*realistic, I would not necessarily counsel you to drop it. First of all, who's to say it really *is* unrealistic? You may have little or no natural writing abil ity and couldn't draw a straight line if your life depended on it. Would I be willing to bet you probably *won't* become the creative director of one of the country's top three advertising agencies. Well, I'm a betting man, so I probably *would* take that bet. But the human spirit is an amazing thing. Who says with the right education, jobs, and practice that your goal, though seemingly unrealistic, couldn't eventually be realized? Even if it weren't, the additional education and dedication certainly wouldn't hurt your career prospects!

What if the goal is realistic but you are simply unwilling or unable to do what's necessary to reach it? Change it. Why kid yourself? While luck plays a factor in many careers, it is certainly not the only factor. The one common denominator of virtually any success story is hard work. If you aren't willing to work hard, almost *any* goal may be unrealistic.

Your immediate and future personal/financial goals will, of course, have a great effect on your decision-making and on the questions you ask (and answers you absolutely need to know). If you're unmarried and childless and someone actually offers to pay you to wander the globe, you may be more than comfortable with the arrangement. But what if you anticipate getting married or having kids in a year or two? What if you know you have to prepare to take care of an older relative?

Your financial needs may dramatically change. The kind of hours, travel, etc., you're willing to take on now may need to be radically overhauled. You may not mind relocating once a year *now*, but resist relocating at all after you've settled down. If you have chosen a job/career/industry/company in which declining to relocate may mean the *end* of your job/career, your future plans must be part of your current equation.

Show me the money!

What is your current standard of living, and are you happy with it?

Can you comfortably afford your current lifestyle, or are you living beyond your means with nothing in the bank and a fistful of maxed-out credit cards?

Can you live on what the company wants to pay you?

What standard of living do you aspire to in two years? Five? Ten?

What salary (or package) is required to meet these targets?

Besides salary, what benefits or package components do you consider essential? Nice? Unnecessary?

Answering these questions is obviously important. You have to realistically define your financial wants and needs. How can you know how much you need if you can't figure out how to live on what you've got right now? Develop a budget. Develop a financial plan.

As you analyze the cost of some of your long-range planning, you're going to shock yourself. Especially if you are a recent college graduate, laying out what "real life" costs could be daunting. But don't forget to look at the other side of the coin—what you're going to earn. Even if your starting salary were $25,000 and you never got a better job or a raise (and leaving out the "costs" of inflation, which is just a pain in the butt anyway), if you work for 40 years, you'll earn $1 million. Earn, on average, $50,000 a year and you'll earn $2 million. And if you quickly ascend to that $100,000 a year level? That's right—$4 million or more 40 years from now.

If you are (hopefully) given the choice between two or more jobs, you need some basis on which to decide between them. If one job pays substantially less than the other, but is much closer to your "ideal" career path, has more promise, and so on, you really need to know whether you can afford to take it...because you very much might *want* to take it, despite the lower pay.

You need to look farther into the future than "tomorrow." Companies still do survive and thrive, and a company you're considering (especially if it is a non-tech behemoth that's been a Fortune 500 company for decades) may very well be around when your grandkids are reading this book. What does this mean in terms of your job hunt? Your financial prospects at that firm two, five, or even ten years in the future may be very relevant indeed. Taking a position that pays less than you would like at a company where you believe (based on your research, conversations, maybe even promises from the interviewer) your financial goals could well be reached or even exceeded farther down the line may be a smart move. And the bigger the company, the more likely there will be significant opportunities to change jobs, even areas (hence, careers) without leaving the company.

What if you are offered more, perhaps *substantially* more, rather than less? Simple question: What will you earn if you're fired or quit after a month, or three or six? Isn't that a reality you need to at least consider?

If you choose a job purely because it pays substantially more—and the job (or the company!) evaporates after a month, or two or three—what have you actually made? A heck of a lot less than you thought you were getting! Not to mention that you are now out of a job. How much are you losing while you find another job? Yep. More than the difference in salary on which your supposedly well-thought-out decision was based.

There's more to life than money, and money is only one aspect to consider about a job offer. Make sure you know enough about who you are, where you want to go, what you need, and what you want, so you're ready to make an *informed* decision, not just a comparison of dollars and cents.

This is not your grandfather's job market (or, for that matter, your mother's). There is no security. Do you remember (or have you heard about) those days when you took a job and could count on reasonable raises for 40 years or so until you retired with your gold watch? Those days are long gone, so making a decision to take a job that does not really fulfill your long-term goals (maybe not even many of your short-term goals) just because it pays more money (even a lot more money) is not necessarily smart.

Interestingly, keeping money in this kind of perspective ties in nicely with the Five o'clock Club's notion of creating a "40-year vision" of your career. If you read any of the books by its founder, Kate Wendleton, you will see how often her members choose between three, five, or more offers and often wind up taking the one that pays the least in the short run. This is not because each of them has decided that money is not as important as some of the other factors we've been discussing. In many cases, it's because they had a clear vision of the financial *potential* of each offer and made a more long-term decision.

Besides, I doubt there are many people who have fervently proclaimed on their deathbeds, *"I wish I had just worked harder"* or *"I just wish I had made another sale."* Always give personal goals the same weight as career/professional goals unless you have consciously decided to do otherwise. Most of us don't consciously decide anything of the sort; we just let the professional goals overwhelm the personal. We "become our jobs"—not inherently a bad thing, but not a good one if it throws the rest of our lives completely out of balance.

Be careful how many of your decisions in life, including, of course, where you work, are based solely on money. The older I get, the more I see how many of the decisions I've had to make have been based far too much on money (either wanting or not having it) and not nearly enough on conscious lifestyle choices.

Money may not be the root of all evil, but it can certainly be considered the root of one heck of a lot of dissatisfaction. There are, at the risk of sounding simplistic, many people without what many of us would consider "a lot of money" (define with your own number of zeros) who are quite content in their lives, thank you very much. And of course there are the plethora of "poor little rich kids" whose inherited zillions have brought them nothing but grief. So keep money in its place. It's important, even essential, but it ain't all there is.

Are you moving too fast?

Don't be too ready to give up what you already have—your current job, whatever its deficiencies—just because you believe the grass has to be greener "over there." Ask yourself some smart questions first:

Can you achieve your ultimate career path in your current company?

How does your current job differ from your ideal job?

What specific skills and experience do you need to transform one into the other?

How can you transfer skills you already have to a completely different career?

How would you describe your absolute dream job? Where would you be? What would you be doing? Who would you be working with/for? What would you be earning?

What additional education or training would you need to achieve this dream job? If you obtained the education or training but *didn't* attain the dream job, how do you think your current job or career path would be affected?

You may be putting the cart before the horse if you're ready to schedule interviews at other companies before asking yourself these important questions. You already have (one hopes) a good reputation at your current job. A good history. Friends. Experience. Respect. If all of that is true, you should want to move on only if your answers to the above questions are negative.

If there is *any* way to stay at your current job and/or at your current company if the answers are *positive*, think long and hard about why you would want to make a change. My advice would be to evaluate what you would need to do to create your ideal job *at your current company*, even if you hate your current job, boss, or situation. Analyze first what it would take to make you happy. And if you can fathom *any* way to do it without going through the job-search process, do so. It's a jungle out there, and better the frying pan you're already in than throwing yourself upon someone else's pyre.

Of course, this is a moot point if, having done the analysis, you conclude there is simply no viable way to get even remotely close to your ideal job at a compensation level that you need. Or if the very nature of the company (ten employees, a field you want to desert, a boss making your life miserable) makes it impossible.

But don't be afraid to ask the questions raised at the beginning of this section and, perhaps, two more:

> **Are there any training programs available that may make the kind of move you want possible?**

> **Presuming there *is* "room at the top," what specifically would you have to do to earn the job title/salary/responsibilities you want? *Can* you do it? Within a time frame you deem reasonable?**

By taking a more patient approach, you may give yourself the best of both possible worlds—working toward your goals at your *present* company while still testing the waters at others.

By the time you finish the exercises in this chapter, you should be ready to sit down and describe not just the companies you'd like to work for, but your duties and responsibilities, your new boss's personality, the people you will be working with, and where you'd like to be two, five, ten...yes, even 40 years down the road. If you have honestly and completely answered the questions you asked of yourself, I think you will be.

CHAPTER 3

Questions to Ask During Your Research

Research is an essential first step in any job search. If you know nothing about the firm, department, job, or boss, you have no real clue of how to "position" your answers to any of the interviewer's questions (or "target" your own questions). That's why you can't just go in with a bunch of basic questions that you could have easily answered yourself after a few hours online.

You have many skills and qualifications and talents, some or all of which may be pertinent, one of which may be key. How do you know?

So the research is not just to give you a set of questions to ask. It's to help you customize those questions and target your answers to the interviewer's questions.

Here's a complete checklist of the facts you should know about each company at which you schedule an interview:

The basics

1. Directions to the office you're visiting

2. Headquarters location (if different)

3. Some idea of domestic and international branches

4. Relative size (compared to other companies in the field)

5. Annual billings, sales, and/or income (last two years)

6. Subsidiary companies; specialized divisions

7. Departments (overall structure)

8. Major accounts, products, or services

9. Major competitors

The not-so-basics

1. History of the firm (specialties, honors, awards, famous names)

2. Names, titles, and backgrounds of top management

3. Existence (and type) of training programs

4. Relocation policy

5. Relative salaries (compared to other companies in field or by size)

6. Recent developments concerning the company and its products or services

7. Everything you can learn about the career, likes, and dislikes of the person(s) interviewing you

Where to start looking

For a very broad overview of any industry, consult the U.S. Bureau of Labor Statistics (*http://stats.bls.gov*) which uses business and economic trends and changing demographics to chart expected growth in employment for occupations in every industry over a ten-year period. The most current edition of the *Occupational Outlook Handbook* is available here, as are online quarterly updates, a wealth of industry and economic information, and the most current edition of *The Career Guide to Industries*, the companion to the *OOH*.

In addition, here's a core list of research sources, many of which should be available at your local library, luckily, since most of them cost thousands of dollars. (Some may still be available in print editions; most have transitioned to online databases.)

> *The Encyclopedia of Business Information Sources* lists some 25,000 sources on more than a thousand specific subjects, including directories, associations, and more. The annual *Directories in Print* organizes companies by industry. *Business Rankings*, also an annual, includes details on the nation's top 7,500 firms. (All titles are published by Gale, a division of Cengage Learning.)

> *LexisNexis Corporate Affiliations* bills itself as the "online business database on the companies that drive global business," listing more than one million firms and information on 1.7 million executives.

> *Dun and Bradstreet's* (D&B) 5-volume *Million Dollar Directory* features detailed information on 14 million U.S. companies. The company also produces hundreds of publications or online databases on local, regional, and international business.

> The 8-volume *Ward's Business Directory of U.S. and Private Companies* includes listings of nearly 100,000 companies, the majority of them privately held, and details that are usually most difficult to acquire about them, such as number of employees, annual sales, etc.

Redbooks.com is a database that includes the information previously available in the *Standard Directory of Advertisers* (once known as the *Advertiser Red Book*, because of its bright red cover) and *Standard Directory of Advertising Agencies*—data on 15,000 advertisers, 10,000 ad agencies, 200,000 key contacts and 100,000 brands.

The Fortune 500 is an annual compilation by *Fortune* magazine of the top U.S. businesses, ranked by sales. It will become particularly important later in your search, when you're targeting specific companies. At that time, it will enable you to analyze not only where a particular company ranks in the overall U.S. economy, but also whether it is falling or on the rise and how it measures up against other companies in its field.

Two other less obvious resources deserve to be mentioned: *The Oxbridge Directory of Newsletters* details 13,000 U.S. and Canadian newsletters in 255 categories. A newsletter may well provide more current insider information unavailable in other publications or databases. And *Eventseye.com* lists more than 10,000 trade shows held at 2,000 venues in more than a thousand cities in 137 countries. Why not consider attending some to learn more about the companies and products out there?

Become acquainted with a key reference resource—the various volumes of the *Standard Rate and Data Service (SRDS)*, all of which are now available online in most libraries. The Business Publications volume details, by industry, the thousands of business (or trade) magazines currently being published.

Such trade publications are prime sources of information, especially if you are relatively new to the job market. Start reading them regularly (many are collected in metropolitan public libraries). Write for recent issues of the leading publications in the fields you've targeted. If you make reading a weekly practice, you will accomplish a number of important goals. You'll begin to absorb information about:

▶ The industry as a whole

▶ Major companies in the field

▶ Trends, new products, and the general outlook for specific product categories

▶ Major players in the industry—both companies and individuals

▶ Industry/professional jargon or "buzzwords"

In addition, published interviews with leading practitioners in the field will give you insight on how they approach their specific jobs.

Finally, there are the major newspapers and magazines you should turn to now and then to complete your research: *The Wall Street Journal, Barron's, Business Week, Fortune, Forbes, Industry Week, Nation's Business,* and *Inc.*, as well as the pertinent trade magazines in your field.

Finding information on smaller companies

A majority of new jobs are created by small companies, but you may not learn much about them in the standard reference resources listed earlier. If your initial research proves fruitless or only marginally productive, try the following outside sources of information:

▶ The **chamber of commerce** in the community that's home to the company or division. You can find out how the company has been performing. Has it been growing or shrinking? How many people does it employ? How many did it employ in the community two years ago? Do people consider it a good place to work?

▶ **Business/industry associations:** Many trade associations are excellent resources for industry data and statistics as well as general employment trends and specific opportunities. Three helpful resources are the *Encyclopedia of Associations* (with three volumes covering national organizations and five covering regional, state, and local associations), *Business Organizations, Agencies and Publications Directory* (both from Gale), and *National Trade and Professional Associations of the United States* (Columbia Books, Inc.).

▶ **Executive, professional, and technical placement agencies:** If you are getting the job interview through an agency, see how much you can learn about the prospective employer from them (and see chapter 4).

▶ **Business editors:** Turn the tables on the news media: Ask *them* the questions! A community newspaper's business reporter or editor will usually be the person most knowledgeable about local companies. They'll know about developments at particular companies, how employees like working for them, and their reputation in the community.

▶ **Trade magazines:** Every industry has at least one trade magazine covering its developments. Call a junior (assistant or associate) editor. Ask if the publication has covered the company and, if so, how you can obtain copies of the article(s).

▶ **School alumni:** A college placement office, your fraternity/sorority, or alumni association might be able to tell you about someone working at the company. Alumni are usually happy to help someone from their alma mater.

▶ **Stockbrokers/analysts:** If the company is public, it will have an investor relations representative who can tell you which brokers and analysts "follow the stock." This means that a representative of the brokerage firm has visited with the company, written a detailed report for investors and analyzed its industry, balance sheet, and management. Call the broker and ask for a copy of the report. It will be objective and revealing, and give you terrific material with which to impress the interviewer.

▶ **Online:** Google anything or anybody and you will undoubtedly get thousands of hits, so learning how to get the information you want quickly and efficiently is an art you must learn. While those of you still in college or recent graduates will laugh at the notion, the less computer savvy may need some practice. There are also a multitude of bulletin boards, databases, and discussion groups through which you can track down obscure information to impress a prospective employer in an interview. Your first step, of course, should be to check out the company's website.

Before consulting individual job-search sites, consider using a job-search engine that aggregates numerous job-search sites, such as:

Careerjet.com—Claims to list more than 40,000,000 jobs from more than 28,000 websites throughout the world.

Indeed.com—Aggregates Monster, Careerbuilder and dozens of other major job sites. Allows searches by city, state, and zip code and provides filters for salary, title, type of job, and other criteria.

Simplyhired.com—Includes millions of jobs in 24 categories, thousands of companies in its directory, and similar filters and search criteria.

Linkup.com—Updated nightly, it aggregates company career web pages, not job sites.

Then consider looking at some of the websites I've listed below. Most are for research, some are just for advice:

6figurejobs.com

Acinet.org (America's Career Infonet, sponsored by the U.S. Dept. of Labor)

Bestjobsusa.com

Bilingual-jobs.com

Bizjournals.com (local business news from cities throughout the U.S.)

Bloomberg.com

Businessweek.com

Careerbuilder.com

Careermag.com

Careers.ieee.org (engineering jobs)

Careers.org

Careerstop.org (provides access to individual state job banks)

Careersushi.com

Careers.wsj.com (including the online *National Business Employment Weekly*)

Collegegrad.com

Collegerecruiter.com

Computerjobs.com

Corporateinformation.com (38,000 company reports from 75 countries)

Craigslist.org

Crunchboard.com

Culintro.com (jobs in the culinary field, from bartenders to executive chefs)

Dice.com (primarily technical careers)

Diversity.com

Diversityworking.com

Efinancialcareers.com (formerly jobsinthemoney. com)

Employment911.com

Engineerjobs.com

Experience.com (primarily entry-level jobs)

Flexjobs.com (freelance and part-time jobs)

Forbes.com

Fortune.com

Guidestar.org (for nonprofits)

Healthcarejobs.org

Homefair.com (to compare cost of living by city and state)

Hoojobs.com (jobs in PR, communications and social media)

Hoovers.com

Idealist.org ("compassionate" careers)

Ieeejobs.com

Internqueen.com

Internships.com

Jobbank.com

Jobsinlogistics.com (transportation, distribution, and supply chain jobs)

Jobsonthemenu.com (restaurant jobs)

Journalismjobs.com

Justjobs.com

Latpro.com (if you're fluent in Spanish or Portuguese)

Linkedin.com

Looksharp.com (formerly Internmatch, for recent college graduates)

Mediabistro.com (jobs in the media and communications fields)

Monster.com

Naceweb.org

Nationjob.com

Nettemps.com (temp jobs)

Newslink.org (a worldwide directory of newspapers and magazines)

Prnewswire.com (news on companies and individuals)

Recruitersonline.com

Reuters.com

Salesgravy.com

Sec.gov

Snagajob.com

Talentzoo.com (jobs in advertising, marketing, and other creative professions)

Techcareers.com

Theladders.com (representing thousands of recruiters)

Truecareers.com

USAjobs.gov (jobs in Federal, state, and local government)

Vault.com

Wetfeet.com

Ziprecruiter.com (searches hundreds of job boards)

Ask the company itself

Once you've culled the *outside*—and probably more objective—sources of information, take a look at what the company tells the public about itself. Check out the company's website and/or call the company's Investor Relations or Human Resources departments to obtain the following:

Annual reports. Mark Twain said that there are three kinds of lies—"lies, damned lies, and statistics"—and you'll find all of them in most annual reports. Read between the lines to learn as much as you can about the company.

You should be able to figure out how the company's sales and profits have been increasing or decreasing over the past few years, what its plans are for the years ahead, and the health of the industry in which it operates.

In addition, an annual report will indicate how the company feels about its employees. Does it feature accomplishments of particular employees. Does it have photos of people at work? Or is it just a series of charts and graphs along with the self-aggrandizing musings of the chairman?

Employee handbooks. Be gutsy. Ask the company to send you a copy of this valuable document. At the very least, the handbook will tell you about benefits, vacation time, salary review policies, and other information you might not want to ask about in an initial interview. It also should give you valuable insights into the company's attitude toward its employees. Is in-house training provided? Is the company picnic a much-anticipated annual event?

Sales/marketing brochures. Knowing about a company's products will help you determine whether you'd like to work for the organization and give you material upon which to base your questions.

Company newsletters. There may be far more details about the company picnic than you would like, but there also might be some personal information about your interviewer, future coworkers, even your future boss. You'll also get a better feel for how the company communicates with "the troops," how they view their future, new product launches, recent awards, and so on.

If you contact the company directly, they may be able to send you an already prepared packet of information, including some or all of the above items. If you request such a packet, what they include is clearly important enough to them that it should be important to *you*.

Although most of us don't particularly relish doing it, homework does have its payoffs, especially during a job hunt. From the research you doggedly pursue on prospective employers, you should learn several important things about each:

▶ What it's looking for in its employees

▶ Its key products and markets

▶ Whether it's hired employees from your school and how they've fared (if you are a recent graduate)

▶ Who the hiring manager is and what type of people she usually hires

▶ Why you might enjoy working for that company

All of this information will prove invaluable to you, not only during the interview, but in helping you get the interview in the first place.

The smaller the company—especially if it is a private, entrepreneurial firm with a founder still firmly holding the reins—the more difficult it will be to find this information. Perhaps that is why the company is still private (or small). We will cover some of the particular (and possibly awkward) questions you may have to ask a founder or sole proprietor, especially if you are entering at the management or executive levels, in chapter 5.

Research from books, the Internet, phone calls, interviews, and the like is all necessary, but don't disbelieve what your eyes and ears tell you if you visit the company. When you're waiting in reception, look and listen. What do the people seem like? Is it a loose atmosphere? Fast? Slow? Does everyone who passes by appear to have just lost a much-loved pet? Are they talking to each other, joking around, having fun? Or is it clearly a collection of Dilbert clones in cubbyholes?

Plan to get to every interview early so you can play a little detective. Talk to everyone you meet: What do you do? How long have you worked here? Do you like it?

Sometimes this "on-site" information will prove more valuable and revealing than days of research.

CHAPTER 4

Questions to Ask "Pre-Interviewers"

The questions in this chapter are those to ask of *anyone who lacks the final authority to hire you*. If you're relatively young and inexperienced, you may do a series of "informational interviews" to learn about an industry, company, or job you think you'd like. Depending on your level of experience, you may utilize an employment agency, recruiting firm, or headhunter. And, even if you know you should do everything to avoid them, you may find yourself interviewing, on the phone or in person, with a Human Resources staffer.

None of these people can offer you a job. But all of them can offer you something almost as valuable: the information about the company, position, and hiring manager you *do* need to land that job.

This chapter will show you how to utilize each of these "pre-interviewers" and the questions to ask them.

Information please

An informational interview should be utilized by someone either new to the job market (i.e., a recent high school or college graduate) or an experienced worker seeking a career change.

There is a huge difference between a job interview and an informational interview. In an informational interview, your goal is to learn as much as possible about the industry, company, and job you've targeted (although such an interview may come very early in the job-search process, long before you've begun to pursue specific companies or even a specific industry). If you are actively seeking a job at a specific company, such an interview is rarely one you would schedule at that company; rather, you should seek out a similar company in the same industry.

If you are more concerned with learning about a particular job description, not as picky about the industry, and not ready to home in on specific companies, then you could seek an informational interview with someone in the same position at virtually *any* company in *any* industry.

A meeting with someone already doing what you soon *hope* to be doing is by far the best way to find out what you need to know before a formal job interview. You'll find that most people are happy to talk about their jobs. I know I often sit down with "friends of friends" and share what I've learned about book publishing. Because there is no immediate pressure on me to evaluate that "friend" as a candidate, I can be more informal, forthcoming, blunt, and relaxed.

You may learn of a specific job opening during an informational interview. If so, you are in the enviable position to unearth many important details about it. You may learn the identity of the actual interviewer (or, more important, the decision-maker) and, if you're lucky, something about her experience, values, and personality. With your contact's permission, you may even be able to use his name as a referral.

As you prepare to conduct informational interviews, there are, ideally, six individual goals you hope to fulfill during each:

1. To uncarth current information about the industry, company, and pertinent job functions. Remember: Gaining knowledge and understanding of broad industry trends, the financial health of the industry and its key players, hiring opportunities, and the competitive picture are key components in your search for the right job.

2. To investigate each company's hiring policies: Who makes the decisions? Who are the key players? Is there a hiring season?

3. To sell yourself and leave a calling card, your resume.

4. To seek out advice to help you refine your job search.

5. To obtain referrals to expand your network of contacts.

6. To develop a list of follow-up activities that will heighten your visibility among your key contacts.

Of course, the line between the people who can give you information about a certain field you've targeted and potential employers in that field can sometimes blur. Don't be concerned—you'll soon learn when (and how) to shift the focus from interview*er* to interview*ee*.

To simplify this process, follow a single rule: Show interest in the industry or job area under discussion, but never aggressively seek out information about particular openings; wait until the interviewer raises the possibility of your working there. You may be surprised at how often the person you're interviewing turns to you and asks, *"Would you be interested in_____ (a current job opening)?"* If you *would* be interested in the position under discussion, by all means make your feelings known.

Smart questions to ask during an informational interview

In addition to any questions your research failed to answer (which, of course, you should now ask), here are some other smart questions to ask during any informational interview:

What are your duties and responsibilities?

How do you spend your day?

How did you get started at this company (or in your profession)?

What do you like most about your job? What do you like least?

What kind of person do you think is right for this kind of work?

What skills are in short supply here? (Careful: This is bordering on the aggressive!)

How can I learn more about this field? Are there specific trade journals I should be reading or associations I can join?

How can I meet others in this field?

What is the best way to get started (in this field or at this company)? (This is a question for recent graduates to ask.)

I'm trying to get in to see people at some other organizations. Do you know anyone at these companies? May I use your name?

Given my credentials, where would you see me fitting in at a company such as yours?

This is probably as close to a "closing" question as you want to get during an informational interview. At worst, you'll get some valuable advice. At best, you may just get yourself a real interview.

Can you direct me to others in your department/ organization/division/company with whom you think it would be beneficial for me to talk or meet?

Now, it's possible that the interviewer will direct you to another person or two for the express purpose of educating you. After all, that *is* what you said you were there for. But there is another positive possibility: You may have impressed him. In fact, despite your assertion that you're "just seeking information," he may be thinking, *"Hmmm, this guy is good He may be right for that opening in Josh's department."* In which case you have just transformed an informational interview into a job interview...with this single question. That's why I like it!

Interviewing with recruiters, headhunters, and employment agencies

Of the many outside counselors who can help with your job search or arm you with job leads, employment agencies are on the bottom rung of the ladder. Dozens of them may get the same job openings from the same companies at the same time. Candidates are a bit like fast food: first come, first served.

Recruiters are a decided step up, although not all of them work on an exclusive basis. So, again, there may be more than one or two of them seeking similar candidates for the same openings.

Headhunters are the top of the ladder, generally working in specific fields (mining, engineering, media, etc.) for companies seeking professional, even executive, employees at decidedly higher pay scales.

The higher up the food chain you go, the more the counselor is likely to know about the company, the job, and the interviewer.

Once an agency, recruiter, or headhunter believes you to be a qualified and serious candidate for a position (i.e., you're going after a job for which you're qualified and, in her opinion, have a reasonable chance of getting hired), you can use her as a great initial source of information. In fact, questions that would be inappropriate or uncomfortable to ask on a "real" interview may be fine to ask a recruiter or headhunter.

Just remember that these counselors are working for the company—that's who's paying their fees and probably giving them dozens of medium- to high-level jobs to fill every year. So, ultimately, that's where their loyalties lie. Nevertheless, if they can supply a key client with its newest superstar—you— their stock will rise accordingly. (We won't mention what happens if you embarrass them on the job or, worse, on the interview, will we?)

Here are some key questions to ask agencies and recruiters:

Can you tell me about the company?

How long have you been working with this company?

The longer they've been on retainer, the more they know about the company and the more they can tell you. And, *are* they on retainer? Or are they just one of many firms that get paid only if they place someone?

Who is your contact at the company? Is it the person who is actually doing the hiring or someone in the Human Resources department?

How many people have you placed there?

Is a written, detailed job description available?

Why is this job available? Is this a new position? Was it created as part of a new project, division, or strategy?

New positions imply growth. Any company growing now may well be one you want to work for!

If it's not a new position, what happened to the person who previously held it?

If they were fired, can you tell me why? If they were promoted, where did they end up?

To whom would I be reporting? What can you tell me about him or her?

How many people would be reporting to me? What can you tell me about them?

What kind of a maelstrom are you diving into? It may be hard to get a truthful answer to this question from the headhunter, and harder still from the hiring manager, but don't walk blindly into a department that's heading for a meltdown.

How long has this job been open?

How many candidates has the interviewer already seen?

If the job has been open for months and the interviewer has already seen dozens of candidates, no explanation is positive. Either the interviewer is fishing for someone who doesn't exist, can't make up his mind, or keeps changing the description of what he's seeking. Or else the job, company or people are so scary, candidates wind up running for the hills. Whichever the case, the longer the job has been open, the more suspicious you should be...and the more probing questions you should ask.

How long do you think the interview process for this job will take?

You know what I'm earning and what I'd like to make. You know the kind of overall package I'm seeking. Do you foresee any problems with the company meeting my financial needs?

Would the recruiter send you on an interview with a company offering significantly *less* than he knows you require? Doubtful. But there's no reason for you to wait to ask this question until after you've already gone through a series of interviews at the company...only to discover that—*whoops!*—he did just that.

Is the person with whom I'm interviewing the decision-maker? If she isn't, who is?

Is the interviewer my potential boss?

If so, you won't necessarily approach the interview itself any differently, but you will certainly spend more time gauging the chemistry between you and the interviewer.

What can you tell me about the culture of the company? Is there anything specific I should avoid doing or discussing?

This is information that is invaluable—a "heads up" that may put *you* head and shoulders above the candidates who inadvertently say or do the wrong thing.

Before you set up an interview for me, could I meet with some of the other people you've already placed at this company?

Not all recruiters will welcome this question or respond positively to it. It delays their ability to get you in the door, a delay that may conceivably cost you the job (and them a commission). So I would consider asking this question only if other answers have caused you to wonder whether you want to interview there at all.

How integral to the success of the company is the department I'd be joining?

A positive answer is especially important to the more ambitious among you. If "your" department is the vital hub of the whole operation, it puts you in the middle of the action and greatly increases your chances to be seen, evaluated, appreciated, and promoted. On the other hand, a "support" department may be less pressured and less hectic...but less rewarding, too.

Is there anything else I need to know that would either doom my chances or help me ace the interview?

It's the last question you ask them. Give them one more chance to reveal the magic elixir that will turn your interview experience into gold.

Why you should avoid Human Resources

There aren't many career books that will advise you to make a beeline for the Human Resources department of a company you've targeted. In fact, most, if not all, will tell you to avoid it like the plague if at all possible. What have these poor (formerly personnel) people done to generate such animosity?

Nothing, really. I'm sure many of them are very nice people who do their jobs very well. The problem is that their jobs have little to do with actually getting *you* a job. They are *not* seeking candidates to interview and hire; they are trying to maximize the number they can *eliminate*. They are the screeners, the people who sift the sands of the known employment universe to discard the unqualified, the overqualified, the under-qualified, and the misqualified. They can say no. And they do. A lot. But they *can't* say *yes.*

In addition to not being able to actually offer you anything more than coffee or tea (and maybe an IQ, EQ, or drug test), many Human Resources departments may have (surprisingly) little idea about what hiring managers really want in job applicants. The more technical or specialized the field, the truer this statement.

I know of a Human Resources director who recommended a candidate for whom English was a second—and not very *good*—language for the top editorial post on a major association magazine. Another passed along a candidate who scored 55 (out of 100) on a spelling test for a proofreading position. Still another recommended someone whose resume was filled with rather obvious or easily discovered lies for a vice president of finance position.

At many organizations, even hiring managers make it a point to bypass their Human Resources departments—bringing candidates in, interviewing them, and only *then* passing them along so Human Resources can take care of the paperwork.

Make it easier for the hiring manager to do just that. Make every effort to get in touch with him or her directly, preferably by dropping the name of a "friend of a friend."

If you *have* to go through Human Resources (and sometimes despite your best efforts you *will),* you can't ignore their power: They're the only ones who can get you to the next level—the real interview. So it certainly would be sensible to make friends with them and use them in whatever way you can.

Staffers in the best departments can and do know more than they are sometimes given credit for. They know the company, they may know something about the job, they probably know whom you'll be working for, whom you'll be working with, whom you'll be supervising. They can steer you in the right direction and help you appreciate the culture you're about to confront.

The personnel manager at a major magazine publisher I worked for was such a veteran. She knew where all the bodies were buried...and who should join them. With her help and input, I became the first person without previous magazine experience ever hired at that company. I paid her back by not only becoming the youngest sales manager in the company's history, but also doing it more quickly than anyone.

Nevertheless, you will probably not go wrong if you presume that the Human Resources person conducting a screening interview has no time to become your best friend, knows little or nothing about the job you so desperately want, and knows even less about the hiring manager.

But it's worth asking many of the same questions you would ask a recruiter or employment agency, and a few others. As always, these are *not* in any order:

What are your recruiting plans this year?

How is your recruiting going?

In other words, are they expanding? Do people want to work there? A talkative assistant might blithely confide in you that it's been difficult for them to find qualified candidates. That failure should give you pause: What do those candidates—the ones seemingly giving this company a wide berth—know that you don't?

What's a key thing about your company you'd like potential new hires to know?

What are the company's priorities? If the answer is just a series of numbers—grosses, sales, profits, ratios—you've just discovered your place in the pecking order: the bottom line.

Personally, I'd value (and survive!) at a company that talked more about teamwork, the accomplishments of its people, or its sense of social responsibility. Make sure the company values what *you* do, or it will be an unwieldy fit, and probably a short one.

Tell me some of the particular skills or attributes that you want in the candidate for this position.

The answer should tell you how much your traits are valued by the company. With this information, you can underline those traits you possess at the close of this interview—to end it on a strong note—and during the hiring interview.

Given my qualifications, skills, and experience, do you have any concerns about my ability to become an asset to this company?

Probably not. If you didn't meet the summary of qualifications forwarded to Human Resources, you wouldn't be talking to anyone. But it never hurts to ask a question designed to uncover hidden objections. (See chapter 6 for a much fuller discussion of this topic and a number of additional questions.)

How quickly are you hoping to fill this position?

Where are you in the decision-making process?

How would you say I stack up against the other candidates you've interviewed?

Can you tell me more about what I'd be doing on a daily basis?

How would you describe the corporate culture?

How would you characterize the company's overall management style?

What can you tell me about the interviewer?

What can you tell me about my boss?

What can you tell me about the people with whom I'll be working?

What can you tell me about the people I'll be managing?

If you're going to be managing a significant number of people, it's unlikely you'd be forced to start in HR, but I've included this question here anyway.

Does the company have a mission statement or written philosophy? May I have a copy?

If not, consider the chairman's message in the annual report to be the corporate mission statement.

Are there any challenges facing this department (yours, not HR) right now?

Do you have a written description of the position? I want to make sure I understand my duties and responsibilities and the results you expect me to achieve.

This is a good question to pose to the screening interviewer (and a great way to ask it). It will help you prepare to face the hiring manager. If a written description doesn't exist, ask the interviewer to tell you what she considers the primary functions of the job.

Watch out for job descriptions that are too general, too elaborate, or too far-fetched. That doesn't mean you shouldn't schedule an interview, but it does mean you have to ask some clarifying questions. Why do companies lay out such god-awful descriptions? Why doesn't the hiring manager take the time to more clearly define the role he wants you to play (and then tell those poor people in Human Resources so *they* can do a better job of screening candidates)? It's a mystery.

What other positions at the company should this job prepare me for? Is that the career track my predecessors followed?

You don't want to blindly condemn yourself to a dead-end job. So find out how you can expect to advance after you land this job. What happened to the person you would be replacing? Is he or she still with the company? If so, doing what?

Try to pursue this line of questioning without giving the impression that you can't wait to get *out* of a job you don't even *have* yet! If you ask it in a completely nonthreatening manner, your ambition will be understood, even welcomed.

At the end of this chapter, I've included an additional list of questions to ask about the company, department, and position. Use it to craft your own list for Human Resources.

Am I overqualified?

This, of course, is a question you really should ask *yourself* before you go on *any* interview. It's essential to admit—at least to yourself—if you *are* seriously overqualified for a position. Many of you might think it's easier to get a job beneath your qualifications: to work as an accounting assistant when you've been a full-charge bookkeeper, to be a receptionist when you've been an office manager, to go back to sales after rising to sales manager.

It isn't. You may have more qualifications than the job requires, but you may no longer have the *specific* qualifications it *demands*. While you may have overseen a 20-person sales force and be known far and wide as an ace motivator, you will have trouble getting a job selling copy machines. Why? Because they don't *care* about your management and motivational credentials. Nor do they need them. They want to know how many copy machines you're capable of selling a month. And they *do* care that you've never sold one!

Employers may question the motivation of someone will ing to "do almost anything." Will such an employee just show up, do what's asked but nothing more? What about someone willing to work "for almost nothing"? To quote another cliché: You get what you pay for. And that's exactly what "almost nothing" is worth.

Especially in lower-level jobs, employers want people happy to be doing what they were hired to do, not constantly looking around and commenting how they could do the boss's job better than he could. The office manager wants to treat the receptionist as a receptionist, not someone who has been an office manager and may, indeed, know more than he does about running an office. Just as some managers worry about hiring underlings who they fear may one day outshine them, many people worry about hiring people for low-level jobs who have already done what their boss is doing. It's disconcerting and, to many, highly threatening.

Questions to ask your peers (future colleagues)

If you actually find a way to talk with your potential peers (and in some companies, it is a normal part of the interviewing process), you will want to ask them many of the same questions you would ask a recruiter, keeping in mind that they will not necessarily be as forthcoming and may be wary of being *too* honest. Nevertheless, their input can be an invaluable part of your decision-making.

Why did you decide to work here?

What were your expectations when you started here? Were they met? How have they changed?

What do you consider this company's (department's) strengths and weaknesses?

If you had to do it over again, would you work here?

What can you tell me about working for_____?

How long have you worked for him or her?

How would you characterize his or her management style?

How are your contributions to the organization measured?

Does the company support you with ongoing training and education?

What do you know now that you wish you had known before you took your job?

How many hours a day do you usually work? Do you have to work weekends?

Do you consider this company to be an ideal employer? Why or why not?

You may be screened by phone or in person

Whether you are preparing for a "pre-interview" with an employment agency, recruiter, headhunter, or Human Resources, your initial interview may be on the phone or in person.

Telephone screening is an effective tactic used by many interviewers. Some interviewers, however, rely on the strategy as a *primary* means of qualifying candidates. For many of these interviewers, the in-person interview is little more than an opportunity to confirm what they feel they've already learned on the phone.

Interviewers who typically fall into this category are entrepreneurs, CEOs, high-level executives, and others short on time and long on vision. Their guiding philosophy could be summed up as: "I have a personnel problem to solve, and I don't plan to waste my valuable time talking in person to anybody but the very best."

A telephone screener is also often the dominant interviewer at small- to mid-size companies where no formal Human Resources (or Personnel) department exists or where such a department has only recently been created. The primary objective of the telephone screener is to *identify reasons to* **remove** *you from active consideration* before *scheduling an in-person meeting.*

Among the common reasons for abrupt removal from the telephone screener's short list: evidence that there's a disparity between your resume and actual experience, poor verbal communication skills, lack of required technical skills.

If you are expecting a call (or calls) from telephone screeners, make sure family members know how to answer the phone. Hint: A sullen "Huh?" from your teenage son or brother is not the best way. And by all means, avoid cutesy answering machine tapes: *"Hi!"* [giggle, giggle] *"We're upstairs getting our groove on!"* [giggle, snort] *"So leave a message, dude."*

What could be better than answering questions from the comfort of your own home?

For starters, conducting a telephone interview has cost you two valuable tools you can employ during in-person interviews: eye contact and body language. You're left with your skills, the facts on your resume, and your ability to communicate verbally.

Don't be discouraged. *Always* project a positive image through your voice and your answers. Don't overdo it, but don't let the telephone be your undoing, either. If your confidence is flagging, try smiling while you listen and speak. Sure, it might look silly—but it absolutely changes the tone and timbre of one's voice. I also like to stand, even walk around, during a telephone interview. It seems to simultaneously calm me down and give me more energy.

You have a right to be prepared for any interview. Chances are the interviewer will call you to set a time for the telephone interview. However, if she fires a question at you as soon as you answer the phone, there's nothing wrong with asking if she could call back at a mutually agreeable time. You need to prepare your surroundings for a successful interview.

Next to the phone, you'll want to have a copy of your resume (which you've quickly reviewed), the cover letter you sent to that company, a list of questions *you've* prepared for *them*, a notepad, your research materials on that company, and a glass of water. You will also want to have already answered nature's call—since you surely don't want to excuse yourself in the middle of the interview—and placed a "Do Not Disturb" sign on your door, so family members or roommates don't interrupt. Needless to say, you never want to put the interviewer on hold for any reason.

Did the interviewer dial a wrong number?

The main rule most telephone screeners follow (or are taught to follow) is *not* to extend an offer for a face-to-face interview to anyone they feel is not well suited to the position or the company. If the phone interview has led them to this conclusion, there are two ways they will try to wrap up. The first is to "let you down easy":

> *"Mike, I really appreciate your taking the time to*
> *talk about your background with me today. You've*
> *given me a lot to think about. You should know,*
> *though, that this is a very competitive position,*
> *and that we'll be talking to a lot of people over the*
> *next week or so.*
>
> *"I think the way I'd like to leave this is that if we*
> *feel there's the possibility of a good match for this*
> *position or for any other opening, we will get back*
> *in touch with you at this number. Does that make*
> *sense?"*

There is another school of thought about the best way to conclude a screening conversation—the direct approach (which I personally favor). It could go something like this:

> *"Mike, I've listened carefully to what you've told*
> *me today, and I have to be honest with you—I*
> *don't think we have a good match here. We're*
> *going to have to take a pass this time around."*

What can you do to fight off either of these brush-offs?

In the first instance, the door has been left at least a little ajar. So a truly aggressive rejoinder is not called for. Nevertheless, you cannot allow the screener to hang up without finding some way to actually get *in* that door—to make him reconsider. Here's one way to accomplish that:

> *"Mr. Billingsly, I appreciate how hectic your*
> *schedule is, but I think we would both benefit if*
> *you could spare me some time to meet in person.*
> *May I schedule a brief fifteen-minute meeting for*
> *next week with your assistant?"*

If the interviewer is a soft touch, the very fact that you resisted his attempt to brush you off might make him relent.

Even a tougher interviewer, though, would be impressed with the confident tone you struck ("we would both benefit"), the understanding you demonstrated ("hectic schedule"), and the modest request you made ("fifteen minutes").

In the second instance, you have to be more aggressive because the interviewer is being more aggressive. Try something like the following:

> *"Mr. Herman, I'm surprised to hear you say that. I must have done a poor job communicating the credentials that make me perfect for this job and my enthusiasm for it. We obviously need to meet in person to discuss this more. Which would be better for you, Monday at 10 or Tuesday at 3?"*

Did it ever occur to you that Herman's aggressive brush-off could be a conscious strategy, an attempt to gauge how you will respond to such outright rejection? If you're applying for a sales position, I wouldn't be at all surprised if that were the case. And if you just rolled over and accepted his brush-off, then the interviewer would conclude you *couldn't* handle rejection (a huge factor in sales) and *wouldn't* be right for the job after all. Respond to an aggressive brush-off by being equally aggressive. The alternative is unappetizing—to hang up and move on to the next interview.

Many personnel professionals fall into a different category—human screens. For them, interviewing is not simply a once-a-quarter or once-a-month event, but rather a key part of their daily job descriptions. They meet and interview many people, and are more likely than a telephone screener to consider an exceptional applicant for more than one opening within the organization.

A primary objective of a human screen is to *develop a strong group of candidates for managers* (the third kind of interviewer) *to interview in person.* To do this, of course, they must fend off many applicants and callers—a daunting task, because the human screen or the department in which he works is often the only contact provided in employment listings or posts.

Among the most common reasons for removal from a human screen's "hot" list are: lack of the formal or informal qualifications outlined in the organization's job description; sudden changes in hiring priorities and/or personnel requirements; poor performance during the in-person interview itself; and inaction due to uncertainty about your current status or contact information. That last reason is more common than you might imagine. Human screens are constantly swamped with phone calls, emails, texts, resumes, and unannounced visits from hopeful applicants. Despite their best efforts, they sometimes lose track of qualified people.

Human screens excel at separating the wheat from the chaff. Because they are exposed to a wide variety of candidates on a regular basis, they usually boast more face-to-face interviewing experience than members of the other two groups. They may be more likely to spot inconsistencies or outright lies on resumes, simply because they've seen so many over the years that they know when a candidate's credentials for a given position don't quite pass the "smell test."

And while interviews with a telephone screener or the hiring manager may be rushed because of their hectic schedules, human screens are often able to spend a comparatively long amount of time with particularly qualified candidates.

However, these interviewers often do not have direct knowledge of the day-to-day requirements of the job to be filled. They have formal summaries, of course, but they often don't possess the same firsthand familiarity with the skills, temperament, and outlook necessary for success on the job. Typically one step away from the action, they're reliant on job postings and experience summaries (often composed by managers).

If those formal summaries are imperfectly written, and if human screens receive little or no direct input from supervisors on the kinds of people they're seeking, you may be passed through the process even though you're not particularly qualified (or eliminated even though you are).

Not surprisingly, human screens often react with a puzzled look if others ask them to offer their "gut reaction" to a particular candidate. Because they're generally operating a step removed from the work itself, their assessments of candidates may be more black and white than gray: Either the candidate *has* three years of appropriate experience or she *doesn't*. Either she *has* been trained in computer design or she *hasn't*. Of course, this analysis may overlook important interpersonal issues.

Don't believe everything you read

And don't believe everything company representatives tell you. Just as employees have been known to "forget" a job when writing their resume and slightly exaggerate their responsibilities at others, employers have been known to tell attractive candidates what *they* want to hear: *"Need your space and independence? Want to work in a freewheeling, open kind of atmosphere? Hey, that's us!"* Except, unfortunately, for the one Neanderthal who just happens to be...your prospective boss.

It happened to my wife. Though at one time we both wound up working for the same magazine publishing company, we experienced totally different corporate cultures.

One reason was because I was in corporate headquarters (New York) and she was based in an outpost (Chicago). I had 400 people around me, including all the major executives and the two owners. She had seven other salespeople and a secretary around her. What *I* experienced as the "corporate culture" bore little resemblance to the reality she lived.

She also had one of the above Neanderthal bosses who, again, bore no resemblance to anyone else I ever worked with or for at that company. As a result, while I was in an environment that allowed me a lot of freedom and the ability to pretty much set my own priorities and schedule, she was virtually a prisoner of the time sheet and subject to frequent bullying rants.

Companies sometimes consciously misstate job requirements so as to attract, they believe, the "higher end" of the applicant pool.

If their gut feeling is that the job requires two years of experience, they may say three are required, expecting a higher grade of queries. They may also believe that the few people who do contact them with only two years of experience will likely be more motivated than the average applicant.

This is called an "enhanced excluder," a means of setting the bar *slightly* higher than they need to, knowing they can always ignore the standards they've set for the right candidate. Some companies use this method almost as a pre-interviewing technique, a way to see which applicants try to get around the announced requirements...and how compelling a case they can make for themselves.

If candidates absolutely, positively, *have* to have particular technical expertise, that requirement should be prominently, specifically, and emphatically featured in the job posting. This sounds self-evident, but you'd be surprised at the number of hiring managers I've spoken to who *don't* specify particular skills they're seeking...and then complain about the experience levels of the candidates they interview. Ambiguous requirements like "good computer skills" will never help an employer attract the skilled people it is seeking. And they certainly won't help *you* figure out whether you're qualified for the position!

An organized list of questions

Here are more questions to ask about the company, department, and/or job. Some may have already been answered through your research, some may be pertinent for the Human Resources screener, some may be more pertinent for the hiring manager. In any case, add them to your list of smart questions!

Questions about the company

Who owns the company?

What are your leading products or services? What products or services are you planning to introduce in the near future?

What are your key markets? Are they growing?

Will you be entering any new markets in the next couple of years? Which ones and via what types of distribution channels?

What growth rate are you currently anticipating? Will this be accomplished internally or through acquisitions?

How many employees work for the organization? In how many offices? In this office?

Are you currently planning any acquisitions?

What has been your layoff history in the last five years? Do you anticipate any cutbacks in the near future and, if you do, how will they impact my department or position?

What major problems or challenges have you recently faced? How were they addressed? What results do you expect?

What is your share of each of your markets?

Which other companies serving those markets pose a serious threat?

What is your hiring philosophy?

What are your plans and prospects for growth and expansion?

What are your goals in the next few years?

What is your ranking within the industry? Does this represent a change from where it was a year or a few years ago?

Can you tell me about your own tenure with this company?

What do *you* like best about this company? Why?

Questions about the department

Could you explain the organizational structure of the department and its primary functions and responsibilities?

To whom will I be reporting? To whom does he or she report?

With which other departments would I work most closely?

How many people work exclusively in this department?

Are there specific challenges this department is facing right now?

What are its current goals and objectives?

Questions about the job

Is a written job description available?

What kind of training should I expect and for how long?

Please tell me more about your training programs. Do you offer reimbursement for job-related education? Time off?

How many people will be reporting to me?

Is relocation an option, a possibility, or a requirement?

How did this job become available? Was the previous person promoted? What is his or her new title? Was the previous person fired? Why?

Would I be able to speak with the person who held this job previously?

Could you describe a typical day in this position?

How long has this position been available?

Is there anyone within the organization who is interviewing for this position?

Where will I be working? May I see my office/cubicle/closet/floormat?

How advanced/current is the hardware and software I will be expected to use?

How much day-to-day autonomy will I have?

Does this job usually lead to other positions in the company? Which ones?

Can you tell me a little bit about the people with whom I'll be working most closely?

Questions about the next step

How many other candidates have you interviewed?

How many more candidates will you be interviewing before you expect to make a decision?

How many other people are serious candidates for this position?

Before you're able to reach a hiring decision, how many more interviews should I expect to go through and with whom?

With whom will I be meeting next (names and job titles)?

What issues are important to each of them?

What are they like?

Are they amiable, laidback, hard-charging? You want to be ready for the personality you're going to face. Won't you act differently with a fire-breathing sales type than you would with a mild-mannered bean counter? Of course you would.

Additionally, you won't want to overemphasize your computer expertise with the guy who is computer illiterate—it'll just make him feel inferior...to a potential subordinate.

How long have they been with the company?

If the interviewer is a middle-aged middle manager at a relatively small company, he's either not the most ambitious person you've ever met or he has "risen to the level of his incompetence." You may want to make him feel more secure—not come on too strong—since he's probably aware he isn't moving any higher.

On the other hand, if you're interviewing with a 27-year-old vice president who clearly seems destined for better things (and higher levels), you'll want to convince her that you're someone she'll want to bring along for the ride, someone who can perhaps make her own rise quicker or easier.

You may not be able to find out the answers to all or even most of these personal questions, but you will certainly get helpful answers to some. *Whatever* you learn will be more than you knew before!

Based on the answers you receive to these kinds of questions, try to create a "model" of the person with whom you'll be meeting—what she looks like, what makes her smile, what makes her angry, how she deals with stress, what seems important to her, what she'd laugh about or cringe at.

Using this admittedly hypothetical pseudo-interviewer, picture yourself actually in the interview with her. Answer her questions. Ask yours. Counter her objections. Ask for the job! Even if the eventual reality bears little or no resemblance to the model you've constructed, doing this exercise has got to make you better prepared than just walking in cold.

All the research, assessment, and preparation is over. It's time for the real thing—your interview with the hiring manager.

CHAPTER 5

Questions to Ask Your New Boss

The hiring manager may not be the person for whom you will be working, but probably will be. Even where others have strong input, most companies still allow managers to hire their own staff, within certain parameters. He is probably a supervisor who has chosen (or is required) to shoehorn in-person interviews into his busy workdays. (In smaller companies especially, the president may be the ultimate decision maker, even if you won't be reporting to her.) A manager who has worked with a number of previous employees who held the same position will bring a unique perspective to the proceedings.

What's different about interviewing with the hiring manager as opposed to your time with a recruiter or headhunter or even Human Resources? This is the person you actually have to impress, the only one who can say those magic words, "You're hired. When can you start?" This is the person you must be careful with.

The hiring manager's primary objective is to *evaluate your skills and measure your personal chemistry on a firsthand basis.* These interviewers want to get to know everything they can about the people with whom they'll be working closely. (As we've seen, the telephone screener may well be an entrepreneur who delegates heavily and interacts only intermittently with new hires. And the human screen usually has nothing to do with the day-to-day operation of the company.)

Common reasons for being dropped from a hiring manager's hot list include: lack of personal chemistry or rapport; poor performance during the interview itself; and her assessment that, although you're qualified and personable, you would simply not fit in well with the team.

Many hiring managers have a highly intuitive sense of who will (and won't) perform the job well and achieve a good fit with the rest of the work group. On the other hand, it sometimes comes as a surprise to applicants that excellent supervisors can be less than stellar interviewers. But a great many managers lack any formal training in the art of interviewing.

Of the three categories of interviewers, this is the group most likely to interpret the interview as an opportunity to get to know more about you, rather than require specific answers to questions about your background, experience, outlook on work, and interpersonal skills.

The hiring interview

Your first interview with the person who will manage your prospective position is not likely to be a walk in the park. You may be stepping out of the range of the experience and interviewing talent of the Human Resources professional and into unknown territory.

And you could wander there for a while.

Why? Experienced interviewers are trained to stay in charge of the interview, not let it meander down some dead-end, nonproductive track. There is a predictability to the way they conduct interviews, even if they utilize different techniques.

On the other hand, the hiring manager is sure to lack some or all of the screening interviewer's knowledge, experience, and skill, making him an unpredictable animal.

A majority of corporate managers don't know what it takes to hire the right candidate. Few of them have had formal training in conducting interviews of any kind. To make things worse, most managers feel slightly less comfortable conducting the interview than the nervous candidate sitting across the desk from them!

A manager might decide you are not the right person for the job, without ever realizing that the questions he asked were so ambiguous, so off the mark, that even the perfect candidate could not have stumbled on the "right" answers. No one monitors the performance of the interviewer. And the candidate cannot be a mind reader. So, more often than is necessary, otherwise perfectly qualified candidates walk out the door for good...simply because *the manager* failed at the interview!

Foiling the inept interviewer

But that doesn't have to happen to you. You can—and should—be prepared to put your best foot forward, no matter what the experience or expertise of the manager interviewing you.

You'll be a step ahead of the game (and the other candidates) if you realize at the outset that the interviewer is after more than just facts about your skills and background. He is waiting for something more elusive to hit him, something he may not even be able to articulate: He wants to feel that, somehow, you fit the organization or department.

Knowing what you're up against is half the battle. Rather than sit back passively and hope for the best, you can help the unskilled interviewer focus on how your unique skills can directly benefit—"fit"—the department or organization by citing a number of specific examples. And by asking a number of smart questions.

What other unusual problems could you face during an interview?

The "it's all about ME" interviewer

Bob thinks he's a pretty good interviewer. He has a list of 15 questions he asks every candidate—same questions, same order, every time. He takes notes on their answers and asks an occasional follow-up question. He gives them a chance to ask questions. He's friendly, humorous, and excited about working at Netcorp.com...as he tells every candidate...in detail... for *hours*. Then he wonders why so many candidates decline additional interviews and only a small fraction of his hires pan out.

I've never really understood the interviewer who thinks telling the story of his or her life is pertinent. Why do some interviewers do it? Partly nervousness, partly inexperience, but mostly because they have the mistaken notion they have to sell *you* on the company, rather than the other way around. There *are* occasions when this *may* be necessary—periods of low unemployment, a glut of particular jobs and a dearth of qualified candidates, a candidate who's so desirable the interviewer feels, perhaps correctly, that he or she has to outsell and outbid the competition.

Under most circumstances, as I instruct novice interviewers in *Ask the Right Questions, Hire the Right People* (this book, from the other side of the desk), *you* should be expected to carry the conversational load, while the interviewer sits back and decides if he or she is ready to buy what you're selling.

Is it to your benefit to find yourself seated before Mr. Monologue? You might think so. After all, while he's waxing poetic about the new cafeteria, you don't have to worry about inserting your other foot in your mouth. No explaining that last firing or why you've had four jobs in three months. Nope, just sit back, relax, and try to stay awake.

But I don't believe Mr. M. is doing you any favors. Someone who monopolizes the conversation doesn't give you the opportunity *you* need to "strut your stuff." You may want to avoid leaving a bad impression, but I doubt you want to leave *no* impression at all. As long as you follow the advice in this book and, especially, this chapter, you should welcome the savvy interviewer who asks the open-ended, probing questions *he* needs to identify the right person for the job—the same questions *you* need to convince him it's *you*.

The "out of it" interviewer

Yes, interviewers have been known to be drunk, stoned, or otherwise incapacitated. Some have spent virtually the entire time allotted to a candidate speaking on the phone or browsing email. Others have gone off on tirades about interoffice disputes or turf wars.

If the interviewer treats you with such apparent indifference or disrespect before you're even hired, how do you expect him to act once you *are* hired?

There *is* a boss out there willing to treat you with the same respect she would expect from you—it's just not this one. Move on.

Time to get up close and personal

There are a number of styles and guiding philosophies when it comes to person-to-person interviews. The overall purpose, of course, is to screen you out if you lack the aptitudes (and attitudes) the company is looking for.

Although experienced interviewers may use more than one strategy, it's essential to know which mode you're in at any given point—and what to do about it. Here's a summary of the methods and objectives of the most common approaches.

The behavioral interview

Your conversations with the interviewer will focus almost exclusively on your past experience as he tries to learn more about how you have already behaved in a variety of on-the-job situations. Then he will attempt to use this information to extrapolate your future reactions on the job.

How did you handle yourself in some really tight spots? What kinds of on-the-job disasters have you survived? Did you do the right thing? What were the repercussions of your decisions?

Be careful what you say. Every situation you faced was unique in its own way, so be sure the interviewer understands the specific limitations you had to deal with. Did you lack adequate staff? Support from management? Up-to-date software? If you made the mistake of plunging in too quickly, say so and admit that you've learned to think things through. Explain what you'd do differently the next time around.

Remember: Those interviewers using a behavioral interview are trying to ensure you can really walk the walk, not just talk the talk. So leave out the generalizations and philosophizing and don't get lost in the details. In other words, just tell them the problem you faced, the action you took, and the results you achieved, without exaggeration.

Which is why composing three or four or more "stories"— actual experiences that illustrate your most important skills or qualifications—is important. Just make sure to structure them in "Problem-Solution-Action" format.

The competency-based interview

You will know you are facing a competency-based interview by the way the questions are structured. Instead of open-ended questions, which give you virtually carte blanche to choose examples and target your answers the way *you* want to, you will face more specific questions, such as:

> **Can you tell me about the last time you missed a deadline?**

> **Can you tell me about your most recent project that included a forensic audit?**

> **Can you describe what you did the last time your boss rejected one of your ideas?**

> **Can you give me a recent example of how you led a team to successfully complete a challenging task?**

> **Can you describe a situation where you had to deal with a difficult client (customer, employee, team member). How did you diffuse the situation?**

Such questions are designed to measure your level of individual responsibility, decisiveness, independence, ambition, and initiative; analytical skills; people skills; and management and leadership skills, including your ability to plan, strategize, motivate, implement, and delegate.

Specific industries, companies, or departments will require specific skills or competencies, what they consider the key characteristics it takes to be successful in a particular position. A bank's required competencies may range from auditing to securities law, from credit analysis to risk management. A large manufacturer may desire someone with skills in cost containment, inventory control, production processes, safety training, or other such areas.

A well-prepared interviewer will have a list of questions designed to elicit specific and detailed examples to prove you can do exactly what her company requires. And you should have identified the particular skills and abilities—your competencies—you know are required and have examples at the ready. If you lack a particular attribute, be prepared to explain why you are unable to cite a particular example that touts that competency. (If you had been properly screened, of course, your lack of such a competency should have eliminated you from consideration right from the start.)

For a far more detailed explanation of how to prepare for this kind of interview, I suggest Robin Kessler's book, *Competency-Based Interviews*.

The team interview

Today's organizational hierarchies are becoming flatter. That means that people at every level of a company are more likely to become involved in a variety of projects and tasks, including interviewing *you*.

The team interview can range from a pleasant conversation to a torturous interrogation. Typically, you will meet with a group, or "team," of interviewers around a table in a conference room. They may be members of your prospective department or a cross section of employees from throughout the company. (A slightly less stressful variation is the "tag team" approach, in which a single questioner exits and is followed by a different questioner a few minutes [or questions] later.) Rarely will you be informed beforehand to expect a team interview.

The hiring manager or someone from Human Resources may chair an orderly session of question-and-answer—or turn the group loose to shoot questions at you like a firing squad. When it's all over, you'll have to survive the assessment of every member of the group.

Some hiring managers consult with the group after the interview for an evaluation of your performance. Others determine their decision using group consensus. The good news is that you don't have to worry that the subjective opinion of just one person will determine your shot at the job. If one member of the group thinks you lacked confidence or came across as arrogant, others in the group may disagree. The interviewer who leveled the criticism will have to defend her opinion to the satisfaction of the group—or be shot down.

A group of people is also more likely (but not guaranteed) to ask you a broader range of questions that may uncover and underline your skills and expertise. Just take your time—and treat every member of the team with the same respect and deference you would the hiring manager.

If you face a series of separate interrogations with a variety of interviewers and are asked many of the same questions, be sure to vary your answers. Cite different projects, experiences, successes, even failures. Otherwise, when they meet to compare notes, you'll come off as a "Johnny One Note."

The stress interview

Formal qualifications are important, but in some jobs, the emotional demands, sudden emergencies, and breakneck pace of work can be downright intimidating—not once in a while, but every day. Even a candidate who knows all the technical moves may wilt under the glare of an etiquette-challenged boss or crumble when inheriting a surrealistically compressed deadline.

When you're interviewing for such a position—whether you're seeking a job as a commodities trader, an air traffic controller, or a prison guard—an interviewer may feel it's almost meaningless to determine if you are capable of performing the job under the *best* conditions. He may well try to assess how you will do under the very *worst* conditions. And that's where the stress interview comes in.

Anyone who's been through one of these never forgets it. A common enough question in this setting could sound gruff or rude, which is exactly how it's supposed to sound. Rather than a pleasant, *"So, tell me about yourself,"* a stress interviewer may snarl (literally), *"So, why the hell should I hire you for anything?"*

How do you know you're facing a stress interview? Here are some techniques an interviewer may use:

▶ He ridicules everything you say and questions why you're even interviewing at his company.

▶ He says nothing when you walk into the room... and for five minutes afterward...then just stares at you after you answer his first question.

▶ She keeps you waiting past the scheduled time and then keeps looking at her watch as you answer questions.

▶ She stares out the window and seems to be completely uninterested in everything you have to say.

▶ He challenges every answer, disagrees with every opinion, and interrupts you at every turn.

▶ He doesn't introduce himself when you walk in, just hits you with a tough question.

▶ She takes phone calls, works on her computers and/or eats lunch as you interview.

▶ He seats you in a broken chair, directly in front of a high-speed fan, or next to an open window...in the dead of winter.

If you are subjected to a stress interview, you may well question seeking a job with a company that utilizes such techniques. If they think insulting and belittling you during the interview are effective tools, what's their management philosophy—gruel at nine, thumbscrews at two?

Don't confuse a stress interview with a *negative* interview. In the latter, the interviewer merely highlights the (supposedly) negative aspects of the job at every opportunity. He may even make some up: *"Would you have any problem cleaning the toilets every Saturday morning?"* or *"Is three hours of daily overtime a problem for you?"*

The case (situational, hypothetical) interview

> *"You're dealing with a publishing client. His printer just called and said the biggest book of the year had a typo on the spine. More than a hundred thousand books have already been printed. What should he do?"*

There's nothing quite like the terror of the hypothetical question, especially when it is a product of an interviewer's overactive imagination. It's your signal that you are about to undergo an increasingly popular type of interview—the case (or situational or hypothetical) interview. If you are seeking a job at a consulting firm, law firm, or counseling organization, you should expect to encounter this type of interview.

The premise is sound: Present the candidate with situations that might, hypothetically, occur on the job, in order to gauge the degree to which he or she demonstrates the traits that will lead to success. It's hard, if not impossible, for you to prepare for these kinds of questions beforehand, which means you have to analyze an unfamiliar problem and develop a strategy to solve it, right then and there.

What most interviewers want to see is a combination of real-world experience, inspired creativity, and the willingness to acknowledge when more information or assistance is in order. (Many interviewers will pose hypothetical questions designed to smoke out people who find it difficult to reach out to other team members for help.) They want to understand how you approach a problem, the framework within which you seek a solution, and the thought process you utilize.

You will have to devote a great deal of thought to each of these questions. If you find yourself caught in this snare, stay calm and use the homework you have done on your personal inventory to untangle yourself.

Here are some tips for handling a case interview:

▶ Take notes on the problem that's being presented. Ask questions about the details. Be aware that not all information is pertinent to the solution. (That wily interviewer!)

▶ Avoid generalizations. The interviewer will want to hear concrete steps that will lead to a solution, not your philosophy of how to approach the problem.

▶ Don't get lost in the details. The interviewer wants to see how you approach the broad problem, so set your sights on the most important factors.

▶ Ask questions.

▶ Share your thoughts–out loud. That's really what the interviewer wants to hear.

▶ Resist the urge for speed; take your time. The more complicated the problem, the more time you're *expected* to take.

▶ There's nothing wrong with a creative approach, but it should always be in a logical framework.

▶ Ask questions!

While case interviews are geared to upper-echelon candidates, candidates for many different kinds of jobs may be given the opportunity to walk the walk—to show what they can actually do on the job: Clerks may be given typing or filing tests; copy editors given minutes to edit a magazine article or book chapter; a salesperson may be asked to telephone and sell a prospect; and a computer programmer may be required to create some code. The more technical the job, the more likely an interviewer will not simply take you at your word that you are capable of doing it.

The brainteaser interview

Microsoft interviewers have famously been known to ask, "How would you move Mount Fuji?" The list of questions designed to assess how creatively you approach a problem—as opposed to the logical approach case interviews are designed to highlight—are virtually unlimited:

- How many acres of ranchland are there in Montana?

- How many lawyers are there in Poland?

- How would you build a better mousetrap?

Most of the same tips I gave you when approaching a case interview are still pertinent—take your time, ask pertinent questions, then talk through the approach you would take to answer the question.

What the interviewer wants to see and hear

What will the hiring manager be looking and listening for, right from the moment she meets you? Here's the advice *I* gave *her* in my book, *Ask the Right Questions, Hire the Best People*:

What to look for: the initial greeting

When you first encounter the candidate, silently ask yourself questions like the ones listed below. The more often you can answer "yes," the more likely it is that you're facing a poised, confident candidate. Of course, no one is suggesting that confidence and social grace can compensate for a lack of ability in the workplace. But in a perfect world, wouldn't you prefer to work with someone who meets all the formal qualifications...*and* has enough self-confidence to interact effectively with others?

▶ Did the candidate grip your hand firmly, avoiding both the "bone-crusher" and the "wet fish" approach?

▶ Did the candidate shake your hand with a sense of purpose?

▶ Did the candidate hold the handshake for an appropriate period, neither too short nor too long? (Three shakes is sufficient.)

▶ Did the candidate use one hand? (A two-handed shake is usually regarded as a sign of over-familiarity, though there are some regional/cultural exceptions to this rule.)

▶ Did the candidate look you in the eye?

▶ Did the candidate smile?

▶ Did the candidate use your name when greeting you?

What to look for: body language

After you have put the interviewee at ease by asking a few rapport-building questions, begin to monitor his or her gaze, physical posture, and general bearing. Use the following questions as a rough guideline, and make discreet notes as the interview moves forward. The more "yes" answers you record, the more comfortable (and, presumably, forthcoming) the person is likely to feel interacting with you.

▶ Does the candidate make appropriate intermittent eye contact with you—neither staring you down nor avoiding your gaze?

▶ Is eye contact broken only at natural points in the discussion, rather than suddenly, in the middle of an exchange?

▶ Is the candidate's mouth relaxed? (A tightly clenched jaw, pursed lips, or a forced, unnatural smile may indicate problems handling stress.)

▶ Is the candidate's forehead and eyebrow area relaxed? (Ditto.)

▶ Does the candidate occasionally smile naturally?

▶ Does the person avoid nodding very rapidly for long periods of time while you're speaking? (This is shorthand for "Be quiet and let me say something now," and it is inappropriate in an interview setting.)

▶ Does the candidate move his or her hands so much or in such a weird manner that you actually notice? (Constant twitching of the fingers—or even worse, knuckle-cracking—may mean you're dealing with a person who simply can't calm down.) Yes, an interview is an unsettling experience, but so are some of the tasks this person will have to perform on the job!

▶ On a similar note, does the candidate avoid shuffling and tapping his or her feet?

▶ Is the candidate's posture good? (Chair-slumpers send an unfortunate silent message: "I'm not even trying to make a good impression." If you hire them, you may encounter that message on a daily basis.)

▶ Are the candidate's eyes usually gazing forward, rather than darting all over the room?

▶ Is the candidate's head upright?

▶ Does the candidate tend to sit with crossed arms? (This may signal either a confrontational attitude or a sense of deep insecurity, neither of which is a great sign.)

▶ Does the person appear to be breathing regularly and deeply?

▶ Is the person's personal hygiene and grooming acceptable? (In other words, would you want to sit next to this person during a long meeting? If the candidate won't make an effort to clean up his or her act for a job interview, what will the average workday be like?)

What to listen for

What the candidate says is certainly important, but so is *how* he or she says it. Make circumspect written notes if you cannot answer "yes" to all of the following questions during the interview. Three or more such notes during the course of a half-hour interview could indicate a problem with social skills.

▶ Does the candidate respond in a clear, comprehensible, and confident tone of voice?

▶ Does the candidate avoid prolonged pauses in the middle of sentences?

▶ Is the candidate's speaking rhythm consistent and appropriate?

▶ Does the candidate avoid rambling answers?

▶ Does each of the candidate's answers have a clear concluding point or do they all seem to just trail off into nothingness?

▶ Does the candidate avoid interrupting you? (Breaking in while a representative of a prospective future employer is speaking shows poor judgment and underdeveloped people skills.)

▶ Does the candidate take time to consider difficult questions before plunging in to answer them?

▶ Does the candidate ask for additional information or clarification when dealing with complex or incomplete questions?

▶ Does the candidate offer answers that are consistent with one another?

As you monitor nonverbal signals during the interview, bear in mind that physical actions and vocal delivery should support the answers the interviewee passes along. A candidate who assures you that he has what it takes to ride the ups and downs of a career in sales, but looks pale and shell-shocked when you mention that you're interviewing other candidates, is sending two very different messages. The "lyrics" may be saying "I can handle rejection," but the "music" doesn't quite support that contention!

Smart interview questions for your new boss

Basic questions

Revisit those basic questions you tried to answer through your research and those you asked the agency, recruiter,

...r, or Human Resources department. If you've gotten satisfactory answers to them, you don't need to ask them again. Whatever questions remain from this first list, ask them. Then add a few more:

> **Can you explain the (department, division) company's organizational chart?**
>
> **Can you give me a more detailed understanding of what my days might be like?**
>
> **Are there specific challenges you are facing right now? Will I be in a position to help you overcome them?**
>
> **What are the department's specific objectives for the next three months?**

After you hear them, of course, you will do two things: Wrack your brain for specific examples from your experience or education that will convince him *you* can help him *reach* those goals. And ask more follow-up questions about how your job responsibilities will impact the company.

Why three months? That's the length of your probable probation period.

> **You and (one of his important competitors) have many similar products (or offer similar services). What sets you apart from them? What's different about the way you do things? What's different about their corporate structure, mission, or philosophy?**
>
> **How fast is the company growing? Is management happy with that rate, or do you have expansion plans in mind?**

Growth can be a double-edged sword: Faster top-line growth (i.e., greater sales) could mean greater opportunity to climb the career ladder faster than usual. It could also characterize a company that spends itself into oblivion trying to buy sales. (See "dot-com bust.")

What is the company's ranking within the industry? Does this position represent a change from where it was a few years ago?

You should already have some indication of the answer to this question from your initial research, particularly if the company is publicly owned. If you have some of this information, go ahead and build it into your question: *"I've read that the company has risen from fifth to second in market share in just the past three years. What are the key reasons for this dramatic success?"*

Alternatively, you may need to ask a question—delicately, please!—because the company hasn't been doing so well: *"It seems the cheese-smothered churros weren't a big hit. Do you have other products in the pipeline you are ready to introduce?"*

How do you see me working with each of the department heads?

How would my performance be measured in this position? How is the department's performance measured? Are there specific metrics you measure? Will my bonus be tied to them?

Probing questions

The previous basic questions, and many of those you asked during your research or while interviewing with an agency, recruiter, headhunter, or screening interviewer, are almost solely to fill in your overall portrait of the company as a whole. Once you have established in your own mind that you are truly interested in the company, you will want to ask detailed questions designed to elicit specific information about the department, the job, and the people:

What are the things you would most like to see changed in this (section, department, group, division, company)?

Are there plans for new products or services I need to know about?

When may I meet some of my potential colleagues (or subordinates)? Are they part of the interviewing process here?

Including lower-level employees in the process proves that the company values its employees' opinions, and realizes that just adding some stranger to the team by executive fiat isn't an effective way to show them how important they are to the company. Nor does it do much for team building or any of those other corporate mantras that get thrown around.

How will you weigh your subordinates' input with your own assessment of my candidacy?

Or (to the subordinates):

What kind of feedback does your boss expect you to give him? How much weight has he given it in the past?

You can never be sure how much influence anyone has with the ultimate decision-maker. I once interviewed at a company where a prospective new salesperson had to meet briefly with each of the seven sales managers, although the vice president of sales was the ultimate decision-maker. Well, one of the two female managers—not the best or the brightest, I might add—was sleeping with the (married) boss. I'm not sure how

I would have ever discovered that (it took me a few months at the company before the gossip reached my innocent ears), but it tends to emphasize the importance of treating everyone you meet with courtesy, respect, and professionalism, as well as realizing that you can't easily discern who is going to be a key factor in your hiring...or your being passed over.

Even if the manager wasn't sleeping with the boss, I guarantee if three or even two of the sales managers had concluded I "wouldn't fit in," that particular VP would have never hired me. Some bosses are more influenced than others, which leads to a good question if you're put in a similar situation:

Are there a lot of after-hours business events I will be expected to attend?

How much travel should I expect to do in a typical month? Are there distinct periods of heavier travel?

Do you have a lot of employees working flextime or telecommuting?

Make sure you're careful not to imply this is one of your requirements, especially if the answer is a frosty, *"No. Everyone works nine to six, and I demand punctuality."*

What has the turnover been in this department in the last couple of years?

Are you about to join a department that goes through salespeople like water through a hose? Who cares about the size of your raise and bonus if you won't be there in 60 days?

How many hours a week do you expect your star employees to put in? How much overtime does this position typically involve? How many weekends a year would I be expected to work?

Can you tell me a little bit about the people with whom I'll be working most closely?

I wish someone had told me about this question before my last job interview! The answer can tell you so many things: How good your potential colleagues really are at their jobs, how much you are likely to learn from them and, most important, whether the hiring manager seems enthusiastic about his team.

A hiring manager usually tries to put on her best face during an interview, just like you. But catching the interviewer off guard with this question may give you a glimpse of the real feelings hiding behind her game face.

If she doesn't seem very enthusiastic about her current team, it may not be one you'd be particularly thrilled to join. This hiring manager may attribute little success, and perhaps a lot of headaches, to the people who work for her. Is that the kind of boss you want?

What is the department's budget?

Who is part of the planning process?

How much budgetary responsibility would I have?

I don't care if you're interviewing for the lowliest position in the organization and the answer is, *"Are you kidding? You can't buy paper clips without submitting a six-part form and getting 14 signatures!"* This question shows that you are willing to take responsibility and understand the importance of doing so in order to move up the career ladder. Ask it.

Can you give me a better idea of the kinds of decisions I could make (or amounts of money I could spend) without oversight?

**How much input would I have in determining
my team's or department's goals, objectives, and
deadlines?**

**How much discretion would I have to hire my
own people?**

**Would I be able to unilaterally fire an
underperforming team member?**

These are important questions for anyone *above* the lowest level; they will help clarify the amount and kind of power you're *really* being offered and give you greater insight into how centralized the company is. If you are at a fairly high level (manager, director, VP) and the answer to the first question is, *"Oh, anything under $100. After that, you have to check with me,"* you may have just learned more than you really wanted to know about the limitations of your power. In fact, at that supposed level, such an answer should send you running for the hills. I know *janitors* who have more discretionary power!

Similarly, if you expect to have people reporting to you, your ability to hire and fire and your involvement in interviewing candidates for your own team should reflect your level of management, but it will also reflect the corporate structure and culture. I once worked for a medium-size trade magazine publisher (400 people at headquarters, 100 more in regional offices) at which only the two owners had private secretaries. Everyone else, including the vice presidents of sales, operations, production, finance, circulation, and editorial, shared secretaries. Even after I reached management level, I was still sharing a secretary with one other manager and three salespeople!

**What would you like to be able to say about your
new hire one year from now?**

What is the one thing I could do during my first three months on the job that would really get your attention?

How has this job been performed in the past?

What do you see as the key goals for the company during the next year? For my department? For this job?

How do you see my role evolving in the first two years? What would be the most logical areas for me to evolve into?

What do you think my biggest challenge will be if I start working for you?

Now, if a manager takes this question personally—interpreting it as *"What problems am I going to have with you?"*—that would tell me something about the manager. Perhaps he's a little self-centered? Perhaps prone to define *your* success by how well you get along with *him*, as opposed to how good a job you do?

On the other hand, she may blurt out, "Roberta" or some other name you soon find out is the "problem" member of the team. *Your* potential team.

Or it may just elicit a detailed monologue about competition, products, services, and/or the economy.

Whatever answer you get should give you a much better idea of how this interviewer thinks as a boss and what he sees as the focus of *his* job.

It's a matter of style

Even if you are comfortable with the job, the department, and the company—and have had most or all of your questions about them answered—never underestimate the importance of your boss's "style," the corporate culture, and how you will mesh with both. The next two sections offer questions to make sure you wind up with a comfortable fit:

> **How would you describe your management style? Would you say that it is similar to others in the organization, or do you consider yourself a bit of a maverick?**

> **When's the last time you got really angry at one of your subordinates? What was the cause? What did you do? Has anything similar happened since? Did you react differently?**

> **On a scale of 1 to 10, how would you rate the work environment here in terms of stress (congeniality, workload, teamwork, and so on)?**

> **On a scale of 1 to 10, how would you rate a successful candidate's chance to advance from this position?**

> **In your experience, are there particular types of people you seem to work better with than others?**

This is a not-so-veiled attempt to "define" yourself according to the attributes the manager cites, presuming, of course, that the type of person he describes isn't so remote from your own personality as to be laughable.

> **What particular traits do you value most in your subordinates?**

Again, tell me what you want to hear, Mr. Manager, so I can tell you that I am all that.

What kinds of people seem to succeed in this company? In this department? Working for you?

How do you define success?

What is your definition of failure?

Tell me about the last time one of your subordinates made a major mistake. What did he or she do? What did you do? How did that work out? What's your philosophy about "mistakes"?

How do you measure your own success?

What do you think your responsibility is to develop your people? Would you cite some examples of which you're particularly proud?

Questions about the culture, chemistry, fit

What have *you* enjoyed most about working here?

What have you liked least?

If you could change one thing about the company, what would it be?

What do *you* like best about this company? Why?

If the interviewer hems and haws over any of these, it may indicate that she doesn't really like the company that much at all.

If she's instantly enthusiastic, her answer should help sell you on her and the company.

The answer to these questions can also give you a good sense of the values of the organization and the hiring manager. If she talks about nothing but products and how well her stock options are doing, it may indicate a lack of enthusiasm for the "people side" of the business.

What is your history with the company?

What's keeping you here now?

What's the next step in your own advancement? Would I be in a position to help you achieve your own career goals?

There are a lot of reasons to ask these question, and ask them early. You'll get a better feel for where the interviewer came from— up through the ranks (and what specific rungs along the way) or from outside the company, for example. How long he stayed at each position—is he a mover and shaker or a plodder? Whether he's even been there long enough to give you an accurate feel for the culture.

The second question is an especially important one to ask of the person to whom you'll be reporting. Again, if the word "people" isn't part of her answer, what does that tell you about her leadership or management style? If the reasons are all financial, I would question her dedication to the core culture...and even whether I could count on her sticking around if someone dangled a bigger carrot in her face.

Semi-closing questions

In the next chapter, we'll discuss in far more detail how to identify hidden objections to your candidacy, how to confront them, and how to ask for the job offer—questions designed to "close the sale." But there are questions a step below (or before, if you prefer), those I've called "semi-closing questions," designed to indicate your strong interest in the position and elicit more of the information you need to weigh a potential offer:

Are there problems that keep you awake at night?

(Follow up) **What could I do to make you sleep better?**

(Alternate) **How could I make your life easier?**

How will we work together to establish objectives and deadlines in the first months of this job?

This is a nice way to find out how much input you will have or whether you're heading into a fait accompli: *"Glad you're here, Ron. Here's the plan for the next three months. Execute it."*

Do my qualifications (experience, education, demeanor, outlook, spirit) remind you of another employee who succeeded at this job?

What are your own goals for the coming year? How do you think I could specifically help you achieve them?

What are three specific goals you and I should set during my first three months on the job?

What are three things that need immediate attention?

What skills are in short supply here?

Are there other things you would like someone to do that are not considered "formal" parts of the job?

What is the first problem I should tackle?

What's the one thing I can do right at this job to assure my success? What's the one thing that would probably lead to failure?

Would it be possible to talk with_____ (the other department heads with whom I'd be working, my team, my boss, some of my potential colleagues/peers)?

Is there anything else you feel it is vital I know about the company (department, job, your expectations, and so on)?

This is the last "non-closing" question to ask. It is designed to give the interviewer every opportunity to tell you anything else he deems important.

A little knowledge *is* powerful

The more research you've done, the easier it will be to incorporate what you know into great questions. Every industry and profession has its own particular jargon—terms and phrases that may be meaningless (or confusing) to an outside. Sprinkling some industry jargon into your questions is a great way to enhance your professional credentials:

How do you think the company will be able to utilize its loyal user base to monetize its recent acquisition of Photos.com?

Your company boasts the highest CAGRs across the entire food industry. What do we have to do to maintain that position?

Your retail deposit base helped you drive the highest NIM among your large-cap peers. Do you expect cross-selling traction to accelerate this year?

In the same vein, the way you phrase a question can effectively show the interviewer how well you've been listening and absorbing his pearls of wisdom:

The job seems to be in a state of flux. Is that your impression?

Although your posting indicated that computer experience was the primary qualification, I get the impression from our talk so far that building a new team is your major concern. Do you agree?

Your company appears to be (team oriented, helter skelter, highly charged, serious, fun, etc.). Do you think that's an accurate assessment? If yes, can you tell me more about how that culture will impact how I work? If no, how would *you* describe it?

Timing can be everything

If the absolutely perfect candidate walked in the door first thing Monday morning, I don't know any hiring managers who would simply hire him on the spot and tell everyone else to pound salt. Even if he was everything the manager could have ever asked for...and more! Why? Human nature: *"I've got to see more than one candidate or I won't have anyone to compare him to. How can I just hire the first person who comes through the door? What would my boss think? That I'm too impulsive? Giving the interviewing process short shrift? A lousy interviewer?"*

The further along they are in the process, the better it probably is for you. Ever watch an ice skating competition? No one wants to go first, do they? (And the champ never does, does she? *Hmmm.*) Why? Even if the first skater delivered a flawless performance, she will never get a perfect score. If the judges gave *her* the highest marks, what would they do if one of the skaters who followed gave an even *better* performance?

What if you're near the end of the process or even, ideally, *the very last person interviewed*? You are the candidate right in front of them—living, breathing, laughing, selling, questioning, impressing. Perhaps they already saw someone marginally better than you, days or even *weeks* ago. Whatever impression she made, no matter how strong, may already be hazy. And there *you* are, saying all the right things, asking all the smart questions.

Remember what I said about how job descriptions are sometimes more fluid and changeable than employers would ever admit? By the time an interviewer gets near the end of the process, the job description has undoubtedly been altered as a result of prior interviews. Whatever unrealistic expectations he had at the beginning have been thrown out the window, because too many candidates proved to him they were wrong. He's measuring you by a completely new yardstick, one refined by all those other interviewees.

They've raised questions in his mind, too. Things he hadn't considered before. So he's thinking differently not just about the job, but about the candidates.

Could one of those earlier candidates now be better qualified for the resulting job than you? Maybe. But if you make a sterling impression and say all the right things, the interviewer may never sift through that old stack of resumes or revisit his pages of notes. Out of sight, out of mind.

When can *you* start?

Questions to Close the Sale

At some point, it may dawn on you that you actually *want* this job. You may even have gotten the impression that the *interviewer* wants you to have the job. At least you think she does.

It's time to find out how real your chances are by asking "closing" questions—highly targeted questions designed to uncover the interviewer's (unstated) concerns, discover where you are in the process, identify the competition, and, most important, ask for the job!

"Is there anyone else...?"

Salespeople know that one of the biggest obstacles to closing a sale is talking to the wrong person. What good is a powerful, professional presentation that generates a series of enthusiastic yeses if the person you're selling lacks the authority to actually buy your product or service? While it may be important to get this person's recommendation, wouldn't *you* want to know you're actually interviewing with the person who can smile and proclaim, *"Great! When can you start?"*

To forestall this waste of time and effort, top salespeople will often use a question like the following to qualify a prospect *before* they begin their sales presentation: *"Is there anyone else along with yourself who needs to be part of this discussion so a buying decision can be made today?"*

That's qualifying! Be ready to ask a similar question yourself:

Is there anyone else along with yourself who needs to be part of this interview so a *hiring* decision can be made today?

If the answer is "no," you can feel somewhat confident that this is the person you have to convince. Often, an employer will answer a question such as this by detailing the hiring process for you:

"Well, Jim, I'm ultimately going to be the one making the decision about whom to hire, but I'm going to have the top two or three candidates interview with _____ and _____ before I make the final cut."

Such an answer would, of course, lead to a whole series of other questions:

Will those other interviews be scheduled following this one?

How long a period of time have you set aside for interviews before you make a final decision?

Do you have a time in mind by which you expect to make a final decision?

At what point do you feel you will be making a final decision?

May I make appointments with those other executives immediately following this interview?

If you properly researched the interviewer and asked the right questions of the recruiter or headhunter with whom you're working (or the Human Resources person who pre-interviewed you), you really should already know whether the person you're talking to is the ultimate decision-maker. In an ideal world, of course. But the world these days is far from ideal. So ask the qualifying question early in the interview—it's important to know whether you're selling the emperor or merely one of his advisors.

Uncover hidden objections

Salespeople also know (or quickly learn) that the key to any sale is filling their customers' needs...or at least convincing the customer that they *can* fulfill those needs. In order to get to that point, however, they may have to handle a series of objections, of which price is only one (though one that comes up more often than others). In order to *confront and overcome* these objections, they must first be *identified*. Needless to say, not every buyer is ready to volunteer the real reasons why he's unwilling to switch vendors, the magic phrase that will win his business, or what he really thinks about your candidacy.

So successful salespeople have developed detailed routines to elicit *hidden objections*—the unstated but very real obstacles they must overcome to win the account. You should follow their lead. After all, you can't eliminate an objection you don't even know about.

Questions designed to clear your path are, by their very nature, a little intrusive, a little pushy, maybe even a little aggressive. But they must be asked.

> **May I assume I am a serious candidate for the job?**

or even blunter,

> **Is there anything that is stopping you from offering me this job right now?**

The interviewer may not bare his soul; he could answer, *"Yes, because you have three more interviews to go if you get past me!"* But at least you'll learn that much.

How do I compare with the others you've interviewed for this position?

How many other people would you say are also serious candidates for this position? How do you see me stacking up against them?

Are there any current or former employees also interviewing for this position? Does the company usually prefer to promote from within?

You can't really knock the competition, even if you wanted to (and you shouldn't want to), because no matter how much the interview reveals about your rivals, you still won't know enough to derail their candidacies. But it's essential that you know how many viable candidates there actually are and how the interviewer thinks you measure up. Invariably, rather than giving you a plethora of details about other candidates, you will hear something like, *"Well, you all have similar educations and experience, but there are some differences in computer skills. As you know, the ability to troubleshoot our system is a secondary but still very important part of the job description."* Hmmm, it might have been described as secondary on the company job board, but clearly it's more important than you thought. Time to sell your computer skills, big time.

Are there any specific areas in which you believe my qualifications are lacking?

Do you have any reservations about my ability to do this job?

You're asking the interviewer for very specific feedback—your lack of a pertinent degree, not quite enough experience, experience with a firm smaller than she would like, and so on. Her answer should enable you to "spin" your credentials so they mesh better with her requirements. Other versions of this same question might take slightly different tacks:

> **Do you have any concerns I haven't adequately addressed?**
>
> **Given my qualifications, skills, and experience, do you have any concerns about my ability to become an important member of your team?**
>
> **Is there anything about my background, education, skills, or qualifications that concerns you?**
>
> **Is there anything else I can tell you that would help you make the decision to hire me?**

This is another variation that I like, because it craftily but directly implies your interest in the position, puts you in the position of "helping" rather than selling, and attempts to close the sale...all at the same time.

There is, of course, a not-so-fine line between appearing confident and being an arrogant boor. Adjust the level of aggressiveness to the tone of the interview. If you've done a good job establishing rapport with the interviewer and are having a comfortable, conversational interview, there's no reason to come off like a fire-breathing dragon when it's time to close the sale:

> **I think we've had an excellent talk, and I'm very interested in this position. Where do we go from here?**

**When can I expect to hear from you? If you are
unable to call me before then, would it be all
right if I call you on ___?**

If the interviewer said he'd call Wednesday and doesn't,
that's not a reason to lose sleep. Everything might be all right;
a phone call the next morning might offer a credible excuse:
*"Oh, Ron, I'm so sorry I couldn't get to you yesterday, as prom-
ised, but I had to put out some raging fires."* So arrange ahead of
time to call him if you don't hear. You'll sleep better.

How am I doing?

**Do you think you will be recommending me to
move on in the process?**

The first question was a successful catchphrase for former
New York mayor Ed Koch, though I think it may come off a
trifle too brazen, maybe even a little too glib.

Here are two questions that are the least aggressive, though
still designed to make the interviewer give you the information
you need:

**What are the key criteria you're going to use to
decide callbacks? How do I measure up, in your
opinion?**

What are the next steps in the hiring process?

There are few interviewers, when asked either of these
two questions, who will not make it pretty clear to the candidates who aren't making the grade that the next step is to
shake hands, smile, and go on to another company: *"How do
you measure up, Brad? Well, I'm afraid you don't."*

Likewise, the viable candidates should be given a road map
for the rest of the process—with whom they should meet next,

how long the process should last, how many other candidates are still in the running, and so on.

Salespeople can be more aggressive

And they should be. Since I've counseled *every* candidate to identify hidden objections through probing questions, ask closing questions, and, most important, ask for the offer, don't you think it's even *more* important for potential salespeople to aggressively seek answers...and the job?

You bet it is. Questions that may seem overly aggressive to an accounting major may appear positively mild to a fire-breathing salesperson. And most sales managers expect salespeople to be aggressive; it's supposed to be their nature. So the closing questions can be as aggressive as you can make them (within the context of the rest of the interview, of course, and with due respect for the personality of the interviewer):

> **I believe I've demonstrated the qualifications, experience, and attitude you're looking for. When can I start?**

> **There's clearly a fit here. I'm ready to come aboard immediately and exceed your expectations. Can we discuss the details of my package?**

> **I'm sure we'll have no trouble dealing with compensation issues. Can we start by discussing a salary slightly higher than you advertised?**

These and similar questions that you should now be able to construct on your own have two things in common: They exude confidence and assume that the job is already won. The latter, naturally enough called an "assumptive close," is virtually de rigueur for any salesperson. But it is certainly a possible means for more aggressive interviewees of any stripe to "go for the close."

Getting to yes

Young salespeople are taught the importance of getting prospects to say yes. Neophytes are often given a series of scripted, closed-ended questions to ask with the sole purpose of getting a series of yeses, on the assumption that if someone says yes enough, he'll fall right into the yes that matters—*"Do you want to buy my product/service?"*

Without going into the plusses and minuses of such a sales technique, let me suggest that there is an adaptation that might be appropriate in some interviews or with some interviewers. Especially, it seems to me, interviewers who have conducted a disjointed interview or even given you the impression that they're a little lost. Perhaps you can help them inch toward a decision with this technique. I've created the following two sample scripts. Until the end of each, I'm going to assume you have done a wonderful job and the only thing the interviewer can say is, of course, YES:

> *"Mr. Barnes, have we established that I have the educational background you're seeking?"*
>
> *"And the breadth of experience you want?"*
>
> *"Have my answers allayed any concerns you may have had about my abilities?"*
>
> *"Am I someone you feel you and your team can comfortably work with?"*

Presuming a series of resounding yeses in response, the sales candidate would be ready to close:

"So should we start discussing my compensation package and make arrangements to bring me onboard?"

Here's a more detailed way to get to the same place:

"Mr. Olsen, the original ad that brought us together detailed a number of qualifications. May I go over them briefly with you?" (YES)

"I think it's important that we review what we've discussed and make sure I haven't failed to discuss an important topic, wouldn't you agree?" (YES)

"The ad specified a BA degree from a four-year college, right?" (YES)

"An English major?" (YES)

"Coursework in creative writing?" (YES)

"An internship for at least two summers?" (YES)

"Two to three years on-the-job experience in consumer magazine editing?" (YES)

"Some experience with layout?" (YES)

"It also stated that the company wanted a 'go-getter,' someone ready to move higher up in publishing and take over the reins of the entire magazine within five years." (YES)

"Obviously, these requirements are just the tip of the iceberg. You want an individual who will fit in with your corporate culture, someone your and my future coworkers will be able to get along with. Do you think I have the personality and personal style to do so?" (YES)

"Have I answered all of your questions satisfactorily?" (YES)

If at some point a question elicits a "no," you would pause, clarify the misinformation, confirm that you now understand each other, then restate the question in a way that would restart the series of yeses. Otherwise, you would immediately proceed to a series of closing questions:

> **Can I assume from your positive responses that I am a serious candidate for the job?**

> **Can you tell me where you are in the process?**

> **How many other candidates would you say you still believe have a shot at this job after talking to me today?** (This is a strong, positive close, one I personally like a lot.)

> **Whom do I need to talk to next? May I set up an appointment with her before I leave today?**

> **When do you expect to make a final decision and fill the position?**

> **Is there more information I can give you?**

Frankly, even an aggressive sales type should avoid being *too* pushy. Pressuring an interviewer for a decision by a specific day (or, worse, immediately) may be going overboard at all but the most Type-A companies. However, if you acknowledge that you're *being* pushy, you may get away with it. For example:

> *"Mr. Barnes, I like you, I like the people I've met, I like the company, and I am excited about this opportunity. I don't mean to come on too strong, but I have been interviewing elsewhere and I am expecting at least _____ other offers before the end of the week. Is there any way I can hear from you before Friday?"*

The nicest thing about this question is that it makes you seem even more attractive: *"Hey,"* you're announcing, *"other companies are ready to make me an offer. What's wrong with you?"*

You can always work for free

> *"I realize you have a very difficult decision to make, but since you've indicated you need at least a week to do so, would you object if I came in first thing tomorrow morning and actually showed you what I can do? I wouldn't expect payment, of course, until you officially hire me at the end of the week."*

Speaking as someone who has hired hundreds, and who still sometimes worries that I've missed *something* and may be making the wrong choice, it would be mighty hard for me to pass up this "free trial offer." It completely devastates the competition! It effectively puts off the decision for a week, during which time *you* will be in the office, working away, making friends and influencing people, while your competitors are, what, sitting by their phones? You have taken control.

Do you really think the decision was being made in a week? Who cares anymore? You have put yourself in a position to *force* the decision to be made in a week. You have closed the presale and virtually eliminated your competition. Is there any question in your mind whether you'll be hired at the end of the week? Only if you really can't do the job or it becomes clear to you and/or your boss that you simply don't fit in. In which case you've saved everyone a lot of grief and only "wasted" a week of your own time.

Questions to ask yourself after every interview

Kate Wendleton, founder and president of the Five o'clock Club, a national job-networking organization, has her counselors ask a series of questions of every candidate when they return from an interview. I heartily recommend that you ask yourself the same questions (and take notes on your answers):

How did it go?

What did they say?

What did you say?

How many people did you see?

How much time did you spend with each?

What role does each of them play?

Who seemed the most important?

Who is the hiring manager?

Who is the decision maker?

Who seems to most influence the decision?

Who else did you meet (secretaries, receptionists, department heads, peers, etc.)?

How quickly do they want to make a decision?

How do you stack up to your competition?

What objections did you have to overcome? Do you think you did so successfully?

How badly do you want this job?

What's the next step according to them?

What is *your* plan?

CHAPTER 7

Questions to Get the Best Deal

Ask a few experts about dealing with salary issues during an interview and you'll undoubtedly receive a range of advice. Some will advise bringing the topic to a head as soon as possible. Others will suggest avoiding the subject entirely, as if getting a paycheck were some unspeakable practice, inquiring about that filthy lucre somehow too indelicate.

Common sense dictates a course somewhere between these two extremes. I recommend that you avoid bringing up the subject of salary yourself during your screening and selection interviews. If the interviewer brings it up, do your best to deflect her. It's really in your best interest to avoid getting down to the brass tacks of salary negotiation *until an offer has been made.* Not talking about salary at some point is, of course, ludicrous. But talking about it at the *wrong* time is just foolish.

So don't discuss dollars and cents until after you've convinced the interviewer that you're the best person for the job. Until you've made it over all the other interview hurdles, the interviewer is still assessing your ability. And he or she is probably still seeing other contenders as well, including some whose talents, unfortunately, may come cheaper than yours.

The interview is a classic buy-sell situation. You are trying to sell yourself to a company for the best price you can get. The company is deciding whether to buy what you're offering, and, naturally, hopes to pay as little as you'll accept.

If you can set yourself apart from the crowd of applicants, if you can convince the employer that an extra couple of thousand dollars would be well-spent on a dynamo like you, then one of the only sure ways *not* to get the job is by hanging a price tag around your neck too early in the proceedings.

If the interviewer is loathe to bring up salary during the early stages of an interview, then your bringing it up is a sure way to make him feel you are self-absorbed and interested solely in the money.

Would you buy something from a salesperson who only wanted to impress upon you how much something cost?

Of course not.

Why would a company hire someone only interested in seeing how much he could get?

I, and most experienced hiring managers I know, have at least one story about candidates who asked only about salary, benefits, and days off...just before they were thanked and shown the door. *None* of these subjects is one to raise when an employer asks, *"So, do you have any questions?"*

Of course, the interviewer may have her own reasons to introduce questions about salary early in the process:

"How much do you want (expect) to make?"

"What are your salary expectations?"

"How much were you paid last year?"

"If I'm going to make you an offer, I want to ensure it is competitive. What will it take?"

Even if an interviewer tries to pressure you into naming a specific number early in the game, avoid committing yourself. Instead, cite a very broad salary range. You might say, *"I believe a fair wage for this kind of position would be between $60,000 and $68,000."* The higher the salary, the broader the range you can name. (Be sure the bottom end of that range is no less than the minimum salary you would be willing to accept for the position.)

You should, of course, have a pretty good idea of what your particular market will bear long before you walk into the interview. If you don't know the high and low ends in your area (city and state) and industry, do some research. Make sure you know whether these figures represent just dollars or a compensation package that may include a variety of value-added benefits.

If you're a woman, make sure you know what men doing the same job are earning. You're bound to find a discrepancy, but you should request and expect to earn an equivalent salary, regardless of what women predecessors may have been paid.

It's important, so I'll say it again: Timing is everything. *You have nothing to gain by discussing dollars and cents before you've convinced the employer that you're the right person for the job.* In other words, the best time to discuss salary is *after* you get the offer.

What if the interviewer blinks first?

You can always tell when an interviewer is paying people too little: She will inevitably raise the salary issue early in the process to determine whether she can afford you before she wastes time interviewing you.

Okay, that might not always be the reason that the subject of salary is broached too early. It might just be that the interviewer is inexperienced or has a premonition that you'll want more than he can afford to pay.

Whatever the reason, if the subject of salary *does* come up too early, sidestep it. Remember: It can't possibly do you any good to discuss salary before you've sold the employer. One of the following replies might prove useful:

> *"I have an idea of the salary range for the position from your ad (or from what the recruiter said). It sounds like a reasonable range to me."*

> *"I'm willing to consider any reasonable salary offer."*

> *"I'd feel more comfortable discussing salary after I understand my responsibilities better. Is that all right with you?"*

> *"From what I know about the position and the company, I don't think we'll have any trouble agreeing on a fair salary."*

> *"I'm aware of what salaries are for this position within the industry. I'm sure that if salaries here are comparable, we'll have no trouble coming to an agreement."*

Fielding the offer

You are a top candidate. You have impressed the interviewer so much that a couple of days later you get an offer by phone.

You're delirious. You want to shout with joy. You got the job!

Don't get too carried away just yet. You've captured the high ground in your search for a job. Now you want to take advantage of that strategic position.

Even if you've been out of a job for months, this is *not* the time or place to let your desperation show, so avoid gushing, *"Gee, this job sounds so gosh-darned wonderful I can't believe you're going to pay me anything! Just give me an office and a phone, and I'll work for the sheer fun of it!"*

I stressed earlier that the interview is a buy-sell situation. Now that the company is sold on you, *you're* the one who must make the decision to buy.

Get the complete offer in writing, with all details spelled out. But be careful: I actually once interviewed someone who was so mistrustful she insisted that I confirm, in writing, that she be allowed to wear sneakers to the office every day...and that I had to notify her 24 hours in advance if I expected her to dress up for any reason. Otherwise, she intended to wear jeans in the winter and a T-shirt and shorts in the summer. And *that* had to be confirmed, too.

Can you say, *"I'm sorry, I just changed my mind about hiring you"?* I did.

Take your time. You should never—repeat, *never*—accept a job the minute it's offered to you. Even though you've probably thought about little else since your last interview with the employer, and have thoroughly made up your mind that you will accept the job if it *is* offered, politely inform the interviewer that you "need some time to consider it."

You could say you want to sleep on it, or think about it over the weekend, or talk it over with your spouse or "advisor."

Most companies will push you for a fairly quick response— they have probably interviewed other promising candidates for the position and don't want to lose *them* if you reject the offer.

However, don't act before *you* are ready. Tell the person making the offer that you need a short time to think it over, thank her for thinking so highly of you, and agree on a day and a time that you'll call back with your answer.

What's the first thing you should do once you've received an offer? *Tell all the other companies you've been interviewing with about it!* Much like the stock of a company that's perceived to be "in play," *your* perceived value to these companies has just increased. Another interested company will know they can no longer sit on the fence about hiring you; it's either act now or forever lose you...perhaps to their competition.

That's another reason to ask the offering company for as long as possible to tell them your decision. You want to give all the other potential players time to get into the game!

Questions to ask when you've gotten an offer

I'd like a little time to think about your generous offer. When would you like me to get back to you?

When would you like me to start (earliest or latest)?

If I have further questions, whom should I contact?

You indicated that my base pay would be _____ plus a quarterly bonus based on specific criteria you've outlined. I understand the medical benefits. You've also told me that I shouldn't expect consideration for a company car for one year. Are there any other items we need to discuss to make this offer complete?

Especially if the money isn't all you'd hoped for, you are looking for hints about how flexible the interviewer (or the company) can be about perks: Is a better title negotiable? Will they pay for your cell phone? Give you an advance against travel expenses? Reimburse your graduate school tuition? Buy you a laptop computer to use at work, at home, and on the road?

As I'll discuss a little later in this chapter, it is imperative that you consider the whole compensation package, not just the salary, when evaluating any offer.

What to do if you don't like their offer

You know the salary range for the job you have been offered. You either discovered it through your research, found out by asking a recruiter or Human Resources, or asked the hiring manager directly.

If you are offered a salary close to the top of that range, consider it a compliment and don't think too long about pushing for more money. You don't have that much to gain anyway, particularly in today's performance-based job market.

But if you're offered a salary at the floor of the range, you may certainly consider making a case for a better deal. You may say something like,

> *"I understood that the position was paying as much as $84,000, and yet you're offering me $77,500. You told me that you've interviewed several candidates for the position. Well, you've selected me because of my management and financial expertise, as well as my experience working with plastics. Therefore, I believe a salary of at least $81,000 is reasonable for me to expect."*

By *not* pushing for the very top of the range in this example, you have made it very easy for the interviewer to see it as a win-win situation and give you what amounts to an immediate $3,500 raise.

Never couple asking for more money with an explanation of why you need it. Rather, always couch such a request within a declaration of the "extra value" the employer should expect in return. Remind him of the cost savings and other benefits he'll enjoy when you come on board. For example, you might say:

"I was able to cut my previous employer's expenses ten percent by negotiating better deals with vendors. I think it's reasonable to expect that any additional salary we agree on will be more than offset by the savings I will bring the company during my first few months on the job."

If the interviewer won't budge and seems to have at least reasonably valid arguments as to why she is intransigent, ask when you will receive your first salary review. If the answer is on your one-year anniversary date, see if you can push for an earlier review to make up some of the shortfall between the offer and your expectations:

"I am very flattered by the offer, though I wish we could have agreed on a slightly higher salary. Could you give me my first salary review in six months rather than twelve?"

This is a rather easy concession for the interviewer to make. He will think that he is getting you for only half the difference between what you want to earn and what he wants to pay.

Look for win-win solutions. If the employer is adamant about not increasing your salary, he may be amenable to a company car or some other perk that works for both of you.

Unless you become overheated and frantic, employers will not be put off by your attempts to negotiate. You will not lose the offer just because you try to get a better deal—your willingness (or unwillingness) to do so may actually be the final test!

Even if you're disappointed, but have decided to take the job, make sure everything ends on a friendly note. Otherwise, you're leaving a bad impression, and may be put under the microscope or on a short leash right from the start.

If you become too intransigent, you may even force them to change their minds! After all, you're already showing them you're not a team player by not giving an inch on anything, no matter how inconsequential.

They're offering a package, not just a salary

If you are already an experienced worker at any level, you are aware that salary is only part of the compensation package you can expect. But even if you are an entry-level candidate, I encourage you to analyze the entire value of the compensation package before making any decision. Some companies provide very generous benefits packages—including stock options, dental care, company cars, free lunches, and more—even to the rank and file. If these benefits don't fatten your take-home pay, at least you won't have to pay for them out of your own pocket.

Most company vacation policies are fairly standard—two weeks for the first three years, three weeks thereafter. Some companies offer "comp" time in exchange for a great deal of overtime. Some match some portion of employee deposits to retirement plans. Many now require employees to contribute something toward health insurance. A number of benefits—such as profit sharing—may only be available to senior-level employees.

You should have learned something about the company's standard benefits package early in the game. If, at this stage, you find the offer abysmal, why are you still considering that company?

If there are any other questions you feel will affect your decision about whether to accept this job, you had better ask them now, while you are still considering the offer.

Here's a comprehensive list of all forms of compensation, which, obviously, is far more extensive than just salary and a holiday bonus:

Basic compensation

Base salary

Deferred compensation (401(k), SEP-IRA, etc.)

Incentive compensation

    Performance bonus

    Sales commission

    Sales incentive plans

    Shares of stock

    Stock options/ESOPs

Insurance

    Medical/dental insurance (Is there a required employee contribution? How much? Is dependent coverage included, or is there an additional cost?)

    Life insurance

    Short- or long-term disability insurance

Profit sharing

Signing bonus

Timing of first review

Perquisites

Accidental death insurance

Child/elder care allowance

"Comp" time

Commuting cost assistance/reimbursement

Company car or gas allowance

Continuing professional education

Conventions—paid attendance and expenses

Employee assistance programs

Employee discounts

Executive dining-room privileges

Executive office

Expense account (with a reasonable per diem when traveling)

Extra sick/personal days

Extra vacation days or weeks

Financial planning assistance

First-class hotels or air travel

Furlough trips for overseas assignments

Lower contribution (or lower deductible) for medical
coverage

Memberships

 Athletic club

 Country club

 Luncheon club

 Professional associations

Paid travel for spouse

Parking assistance/reimbursement

Personal use of frequent-flyer awards

Private secretary

Shorter waiting period to qualify for medical coverage

Tax assistance

Tuition assistance/reimbursement

Relocation expenses

Closing costs, bridge loan

Company purchase of your home

Discounted loans/mortgages

Home-buying trips

Lodging while between homes

Mortgage funds/short-term loans

Mortgage prepayment penalty

Mortgage rate differential/housing allowance

Moving expenses

Outplacement assistance for spouse

Real estate brokerage fees

Temporary dual housing

Trips home during dual housing

Related to severance

Consulting fees after termination

Insurance benefits after termination

Severance pay and outplacement, including extra weeks/
months of severance

Possible restrictions

Assignment of copyrights or patents to company

Noncompete agreement or clause in an employment contract

Onerous policy re: computer or Internet use

Questions to ask yourself before saying "yes!"

Let's review some of the basic questions you asked yourself
very early on (didn't you?): What's the purpose of your job
hunt? To get an interview? Only if you enjoy collecting unemployment on the way to your next performance. To get a job?
Well, sure, but what *kind* of job? How about getting a job that
you will actually like, that you can actually do, that ties in with
your values and interests and offers future opportunities?

Don't get me wrong. There are certainly situations in which you can't be choosy and, indeed, getting a job, *any* job, is preferable to cruising local trash bins. But those situations should be a result of extraordinary events that create emergent circumstances—if you don't get a job tomorrow, your family doesn't eat. Don't "create" those circumstances in your head and convince yourself that a job offer, *any* job offer, is something you should leap at. What good (again, except under the direst of circumstances) is getting a lousy job that you will wind up hating in a month...or less? Do you really want to restart this whole process from scratch? I didn't think so.

So as tempting as it is to accept an offer without a lot of deep analysis, especially if the money is exceptional (or, at least, more than you thought you were going to get), take the time to go through that analytical process and ask yourself these smart questions:

Do I really want this job?

Does this job mesh with my long-term career plans, or is it an abrupt detour?

Does the described "career path" mesh with my own?

Can I really do this job as described? Will I enjoy doing it as described?

Does the company's/department's culture match my strengths? Will I comfortably fit in with the team and/or department?

Do I really like/respect the person I'll be working for?

Do I like the people with whom I'll be working or whom I'll be managing?

> **Is there anything else I need to know about** *anything*—**the company, department, job description, boss, team, subordinates, colleagues, and so on—to assure myself that this is the right move?**

And what's the purpose of asking questions? To get the job by showing how smart you are and how much research you've done? Only partly. Yep, that other part (and don't sell it short) is to make sure the answers make you smile, not wince! A fast-paced environment where merit is quickly rewarded? Great! Just what you want, Ms. Type A. A cutthroat department where you'll need to spend half your time covering your butt and the other half bolstering your boss's ego? Don't think so, Ms. Nonprofit.

No matter how good the offer and how happy you are, don't think only of the present. Make sure you ask the following smart questions:

> **In this job or department, on what basis are raises and bonuses awarded?**

> **Could you tell me more about how bonuses are structured? How much of it is based on my individual performance? What percentage of it is based on the performance of the department, company, division, or some other component?**

Is the job description negotiable?

Remember that you are not just negotiating your compensation, you are also negotiating what particular work you will do for that salary (plus benefits and perks, of course). There is a lot more room to "define" a job the way *you* want than most employers will ever admit. The more they want you, the more flexible they may prove to be.

Why don't you want me?

Invariably (at least once in your lifetime, probably more) you will not be offered a job, no matter how many times you've gone back, how many interviews you've had. There are many possible reasons. The job was more fluid than you thought—the company is rethinking its strategy and isn't even sure they're hiring anybody. Or they're redefining the job (which may or may not work in your favor). Or the executive who has to sign off on the decision went to the Bahamas...for three weeks. Or the hiring manager simply can't decide between you and another candidate. Or two. Or three.

There are two kinds of rejection that occur during the job-search process: the kind you expect and the kind you don't. The first is easy to understand and describe. I once interviewed for a vice presidency at a prestigious international travel magazine. I knew things had not gotten off to a good start when I met the interviewer at a restaurant—he looked like he had just stepped out of the pages of *Gentleman's Quarterly*. And I...well, I didn't. I wasn't wearing jeans and I didn't have nose hairs creeping out of both nostrils, but I was clearly in a different sartorial league. I saw the evaluating look in his eyes and knew I had already suffered one strike.

Within 15 minutes, I knew I had definitely struck out. In answer to a very specific question, I happily noted that I did indeed have the unusual experience he said he needed. I had done it for six months at a single job. There was then a long pause, as he unsuccessfully scanned my resume for any hint of that job...and I realized I would not be enjoying dessert.

The person he eventually hired was a lightweight sales-person and poor manager but a charming rake who clearly owned a monstrous closet full of the latest designer duds. I had severely misjudged the "qualifications" most important to the interviewer, then compounded my error by attempting to "sanitize" my resume to avoid a charge of job-hopping.

A clear sense of sartorial style was an unstated but highly implied requirement for the job that I failed to identify or even contemplate. I just didn't think of clothes as anything more than something you wore because society didn't condone running naked around the office. Not only would I never get a job where model-level "grooming" was a keenly desired trait, I would never *want* such a job.

The lesson learned was more subtle but far more important: Think about the real requirements for the job and make sure they match not just your desires but *you*. If I had thought for even a moment, it should have been apparent that the audience for such a magazine would be decidedly upscale, as would the advertisers, as should the image of the salesperson trying to *sell* those advertisers. I work hard, work fast, and get results, but I am never going to give anyone the impression that I am Ralph Lauren incarnate. Nor, if I want to have a happy life, should I try.

What if you believed in your soul that you knocked the interviewer's socks off? If it comes as a genuine shock that you didn't receive an offer at the top end of the salary range, let alone any offer at all, go through your memory and your interview notes to figure out how you could have so badly misread the situation. Did the interviewer hint that he had a problem with something that you ignored in your haste to talk about something else?

Just be aware that there are many reasons this might have occurred, and certainly not all of them are even remotely connected to your interview. The job description may have changed without your knowledge. Another candidate with much stronger credentials may have waltzed in and delegated you to that sad "Strong Number Two" position. A much-loved former employee may have been welcomed back. Or the president's cousin's son may have needed a job after flunking out of college.

The position may not even have actually been real—the interviewer may have concocted a quick one- or two-day "experiment" to see if there was anyone out there better than the employee he already had. (In my experience, this happens in smaller companies all the time, especially family-run firms.) You may not only have had to impress him more than the other candidates, you may have had to beat out the guy already on the job!

Will you ever know for sure? Probably not. Not that long ago, I would have given you a bunch of advice on how to get the interviewer to give you some hints so you can do better the next time. Unfortunately, the hiring landscape has changed pretty dramatically in the last couple of decades. Employers are so scared of being sued that it's difficult for another employer to get more than "name, rank, and serial number" (name, title, and salary) when calling for a new employee reference. Believe me—I'm the only person in my company who is allowed to talk to someone asking for a reference. And I say as little as possible, certainly nothing even remotely negative. Which is, after all, why they've called me in the first place—to ensure they aren't hiring someone I just fired for embezzlement, sheer craziness, or killing my cats. Sorry, no other info. Good luck. Better you than me. Let the cats out…quick.

If you're working with a recruiter or headhunter, he or she may be in a position to get more information than you would on your own, but, again, don't count on it.

What if you left the interview with the distinct impression that there were unexpressed objection? You tried. You asked probing questions. You all but begged for feedback. And got nothing.

Then following up is even more important. If you know what the objection is, answer it in your follow-up letter. Then write another, somehow bringing up the objection again and giving yet another reason why it isn't valid. And another.

The danger, of course, is that you're tilting at windmills of your own creation, that there *is* no real objection, just some of the above possibilities (vacation, indecision, etc.). In which case, all you're doing is drawing the interviewer's attention to some glaring hole in your resume or education or qualifications...none of which he noticed before. But thanks to your aggressive follow-up, you are now a noncandidate!

After an enthusiastic recounting of how much you want the job, how perfect your qualifications seem to mesh with their needs, and so on (either in a letter or email or during a telephone conversation), here are two smart questions to ask if a job offer doesn't materialize:

> **Is there more information I can give you?**

> **I've been giving a lot of thought to (something you discussed) and have developed some (ideas, sketches, plans, proposals). May I come in and discuss them with you?**

Your negotiating "cheat sheet"

___ **Wait until you receive an offer** before you discuss salary, benefits, vacation days, and so on. Deflect any question of salary that comes up early in the interview with an answer like this:

> *"From what I know about the position and the company, I don't think we'll have any trouble agreeing on a fair salary"*

or

> *"I'd like to know a little bit more about the job responsibilities and the level of expertise you're expecting before I feel comfortable discussing a salary."*

___ **Research compensation levels.** Check within your industry, your city and state. If you don't already know the salary range for the specific position you're considering, find out. You need to enter any salary negotiation armed with this information.

___ **Know your worth.** When you receive a solid offer, you know that the company wants you. They have decided you are the best candidate they have met. This puts you in a relative position of power. If they balk at your initial salary demand, remind them of the specific benefits they stand to gain by hiring you.

___ **Get it in writing.** Especially if you negotiate a complex, nonstandard salary/benefits package. Be sure you have something in writing—either a letter, memo, or email from the employer or one you've sent that's been acknowledged—*before* you give notice to your current employer.

___ **Negotiate the perks.** Make sure you understand the value of *all* the potential benefits in the salary/benefits package. Benefits can vary widely and, depending on your level, could represent a substantial portion of your overall compensation package.

___ **Calculate hidden costs**. Higher local income or property taxes, the cost and length of your commute, the cost of private school because of the poor local public system, and other similar concerns need to be "monetized" and considered.

___ **Shoot for the top salary.** If it is more than the company will pay, the interviewer will counter with another offer. Work toward a compromise from there. Employers expect some give-and-take. You will not make them angry if you remain calm and professional.

Once you've accepted an offer

How do you convince someone who's just offered you a job that she absolutely made the right decision? Ask one of these smart questions:

> **Are there any upcoming events occurring before my start date in which I could participate?**

The more social, the better. You really want to get to know your boss, peers and subordinates once they've "let their hair down." (If they remain stiff and formal even at social events, there's a message there, too!) So a company picnic is great. A departmental Friday night "let's-have-a-beer-together" is nice, though socially tough if you're not a butterfly. It would be most beneficial if you could attend one of these before you make a decision, but that's unlikely. However, if there's a big press conference or similar corporate event, you could always ask to attend.

> **What could I do before my first day to jump-start my entry into the department?**
>
> **Is there any reading I can do to prepare for my first day (reports, memos, whatever)?**

Both of these (and similar) questions will confirm to the interviewer that he has made the right decision. Look at that passion! That interest! That aggression!

Questions That Get Real

In the Introduction, I boiled down 101 tough interview questions to six. Well, I'm going to boil down the many smart questions I've suggested you ask to six as well. When all is said and done, here's what you absolutely want to know before you accept any job:

Can I do the job?

Are you really qualified? Be honest with yourself, because if the answer is no, sooner or later it won't be a secret to your boss, either.

Do I _want_ to do the job?

Your potential boss, coworkers and/or subordinates may appear to love and want you, but you'd better be sure this is a job _you_ can be passionate about. If you are not, but you plan to take it anyway, at least be honest and _know_ you are compromising for a reason that is valid to you...like, you have to eat.

Does this job fit in with my long-range plans?

The more solid and thought-out your long-range goals, the easier it is to create a directed and targeted career _path_ rather than simply a series of jobs that fail to build upon one another. Just as you can and should take charge of the interview, you must control your own career path. Make sure you have honestly analyzed whether this job fits in with your long-term goals.

Will I fit in?

Do you like your new boss? How about the people you'll be working with and those you'll be managing? A job is not simply a set of functions, it's a collection of environments created by all the other people that work at the company. You may be totally qualified for and challenged by the job itself, but if you can't stand any of the people, how long do you think you're going to last?

Can I live on what they want to pay me?

I've lectured you enough about keeping money in perspective, but one does have to live. If your ideal job won't even pay the rent or the mortgage, you have a problem. But the biggest problem is if you haven't bothered to think about your financial needs at all.

Do I feel secure taking a job at_____?

Doubling your salary may be wonderful. Stock options could make you rich. Or you could find yourself back on the street in a month if you haven't bothered to ask yourself this question. Always evaluate the compensation package in concert with your analysis of the health of the company. It doesn't matter how much they promise to pay you if they're heading toward bankruptcy.

APPENDIX

All the Smart Questions to Ask

About the company

Are you currently planning any acquisitions?

Do you have a lot of employees working flextime or telecommunting?

How rapidly is the company growing?

How many employees work for the organization?

Is there anything else you feel it is vital I know about the company (or department, job, your expectations, and so on)?

On a scale of 1 to 10, how would you rate the work environment here in terms of stress (congeniality, workload, teamwork, and so on)?

Can you explain the company's organizational chart?

What are the company's strengths and weaknesses?

What are your goals for the next few years?

What are your key markets? Are they growing?

What are your leading products or services?

What are your prospects and plans for growth and expansion?

What do you like best about this company? Why?

What do you see as key goals for the company during the next year?

What growth rate are you currently anticipating? Will this be accomplished internally or through acquisitions?

What has been your layoff history in the last five years? Do you anticipate any cutbacks in the near future? If you do, how will they impact my department or position?

What is your hiring philosophy?

What is your ranking within the industry? Does this represent a change from where it was a year or a few years ago?

What is your share of each of your markets?

What major problems or challenges have you recently faced? How were they addressed? What results do you expect?

What products or services are you planning to introduce in the near future?

Which other company serving your markets poses a serious threat?

Who owns the company?

Will you be entering any new markets in the next couple of years? Which ones and via what types of distribution channels?

About the department

Are there specific challenges you are facing right now?

Can you tell me about a successful project and how you managed it?

Can you tell me about some recent problems you've faced and how you (as a team) overcame them?

Can you explain the organizational structure of the department and its primary functions and responsibilities?

How is the department's performance measured?

How many people work exclusively in this department?

If you could change one thing about the way this department works (or is structured, managed, compensated, and so on), what would it be?

To whom does my boss report?

To whom will I be reporting?

What are the department's specific objectives for the next three months?

What are the department's strengths and weaknesses?

What are the department's current goals and objectives?

What has the turnover been in this department in the last couple of years?

What is the department's budget? Who is part of the planning process?

What was the last great challenge faced by the department? How did you and your team handle it?

What would you most like to see changed in this department?

With which other departments would I work most closely?

About the Job

Are there a lot of after-hours business events I will be expected to attend?

101 Smart Questions to Ask on Your Interview |

Are there other things you would like someone to do that are not considered "formal" parts of the jobs?

Can you give me a better idea of the kinds of decisions I could make (or amounts of money I could spend) without oversight?

Could you describe a typical day in this position?

Does this job usually lead to other positions in the company? Which ones?

How advanced or current is the hardware and software I will be expected to use?

How did this job become available? Was the previous person promoted? What is his or her new title? Was the previous person fired? Why?

How do you see me working with each of the department heads?

How do you see my role evolving in the first two years?

How has this job been performed in the past?

How long has this position been available?

How many hours per week do you expect your star employees to put in?

How many people will be reporting to me?

How much budgetary responsibility would I have?

How much day-to-day autonomy would I have?

How much discretion would I have to hire my own people?

How much input would I have in determining my team's or department's goals, objectives, and deadlines?

How much travel should I expect to do in a typical month?

How will we work together to establish objectives and deadlines in the first months of this job?

How would my performance be measured?

Is a written job description available?

Is relocation an option, a possibility, or a requirement?

Is there anyone within the organization who is interviewing for this position?

On a scale of 1 to 10, how would you rate a successful candidate's chance to advance from this position?

On what basis are raises and bonuses awarded?

Please tell me a little bit about the people with whom I'll be working most closely.

Please tell me more about your training programs: Do you offer reimbursement for job-related education? Time off?

What are three specific goals I should set for my first three months on the job?

What three things need immediate attention?

What do you think my biggest challenge will be?

What is the first problem I should tackle?

What is the one thing I should do during my first three months on the job?

What kind of training should I expect and for how long?

What skills are in short supply here?

What will my days be like?

What would be the most logical areas for me to evolve into?

What would you like to be able to say about your new hire one year from now?

Where will I be working? May I see it?

Would I be able to speak with the person who held this job previously?

Would I be able to unilaterally fire an underperforming team member?

About the process (including "closing" questions)

Are there any current or former employees interviewing for this position? Does the company usually prefer to promote from within?

Are there any specific areas in which you believe my qualifications are lacking?

Before you're able to reach a hiring decision, how many more interviews should I expect to go through and with whom?

Can we discuss the details of my package?

Can you tell me where you are in the process?

Do you have any concerns I haven't adequately addressed?

Do you have any reservations about my ability to do this job?

Do you think you will be recommending me to move on in the process?

How am I doing?

How do I compare with the others you have interviewed for this position?

How many other candidates have you interviewed? How many more will you be interviewing before you expect to make a decision?

How many other people would you say are also serious candidates for this position?

How much time have you set aside for interviews before you make a final decision?

How will you weight your subordinates' input?

Is there anything else I can tell you that would help you make the decision to hire me?

Is there anything else about my background, education, skills, or qualifications that concerns you?

Is there anything that is stopping you from offering me this job right now?

Is there more information I can give you?

May I assume I am a serious candidate for the job?

Over what period of time will additional interviews take place?

What are the key criteria you are going to use to decide callbacks?

What are the next steps in the hiring process?

When can I expect to hear from you?

When can I start?

When do you expect to make a final decision and fill the position?

When may I meet some of my potential colleagues (or subordinates)?

Where do we go from here?

Whom do I need to talk to next?

With whom will I be meeting next (names and job titles)?

About upcoming interviewers

How long have they been with the company?

What are they like?

What issues are important to each of them?

With whom will I be meeting next (names and job titles)?

About your boss's "style"

How do you define success?

How do you measure your own success?

How often do you and your team socialize outside of work?

How would you describe your management style?

In your experience, are there particular types of people you seem to work better with than others?

What do you think your responsibility is to develop your people?

What's your definition of failure?

What kinds of people seem to succeed in this company? In this department? Working for you?

What particular traits do you value most in your subordinates?

What's your philosophy about "mistakes"?

When's the last time you got really angry at one of your subordinates? What was the cause? What did you do?

After every interview

How badly do you want this job?

How did it go?

How do you stack up to your competition?

How many people did you see?

How much time did you spend with each interviewer?

How quickly do they want to make a decision?

What did they say?

What did you say?

What's the next step, according to them?

What is *your* plan?

What objections did you have to overcome? Do you think you did so successfully?

What role does each person (with whom you interviewed) play?

Who else did you meet (secretaries, receptionists, department heads, peers, and so on)?

Who is the decision-maker?

Who is the hiring manager?

Who seemed the most important?

Who seems to most influence the decision?

After receiving an offer

Are there any other items we need to discuss to make this offer complete?

Are there any upcoming events occurring before my start date in which I could participate?

If I have further questions, whom should I contact?

Is there any reading I can do to prepare for my first day?

What could I do before my first day to jump-start my entry into the department?

When would you like me to get back to you?

When would you like me to start?

Agencies and recruiters

Could I meet with some of the other people you've placed at this company?

Do you foresee any problems with the company meeting my financial needs?

How integral to the company's success is the department I'd be joining?

How long do you think the interview process for this job will take?

How long has this job been open?

How long have you been working with this company?

How many candidates has the interviewer already seen?

How many people have you placed at this company?

How many people would be reporting to me?

Is a written, detailed job description available?

Is the interviewer my potential boss?

Is the person with whom I'm interviewing the decision-maker? If not, who is?

Is there anything specific I should avoid doing or discussing?

Is this a new position? Was it created as part of a new project, division, or strategy?

Can you tell me about the company?

To whom would I be reporting?

What can you tell me about the culture of the company?

What else do I need to know?

What happened to the person who previously held this position?

Who is your contact at the company?

Why is this job available?

Before you accept an fffer

Can I really do this job as described? Will I enjoy doing it as described?

Do I like the people with whom I'll be working or whom I'll be managing?

Do I really like/respect the person I'll be working for?

Do I really want this job?

Does the company's/department's culture match my strengths? Will I comfortably fit in with the team and/or department?

Does the described "career path" mesh with my own?

Does the job mesh with my long-term career plans, or is it an abrupt detour?

During an Informational Interview

Can you direct me to others at your organization whom you think I should meet?

Do you know anyone at the organizations I've targeted?

Given my credentials, where would you see me fitting in at a company such as yours?

How can I learn more about this field?

How can I meet others in this field?

How did you get started at this company (or in your profession)?

How do you spend your day?

What are your duties and responsibilities?

What do you like least about your job?

What do you like most about your job?

What is the best way to get started (in this field or at this type of company)?

What kind of person do you think is right for this kind of work?

What skills are in short supply here?

Human Resources

Am I overqualified for this position?

Are there any challenges facing the department right now?

Can you tell me more about what I'd be doing on a daily basis?

Do you have a written description of the position?

Do you have any concerns about my ability to become an asset to this company?

Does the company have a mission statement or written philosophy?

How quickly are you hoping to fill this position?

How would you characterize the company's overall management style?

How would you describe the corporate culture?

How would you say I stack up against the other candidates you've interviewed?

Can you tell me some of the particular skills or attributes that you want in the candidate for this position?

What are your recruiting plans this year? How is your recruiting going?

What can you tell me about my boss?

What can you tell me about the interviewer?

What can you tell me about the people I'll be managing?

What can you tell me about the people with whom I'll be working?

What's a key thing about your company you'd like potential new hires to know?

What other positions at the company should this job prepare me for?

Where are you in the decision-making process?

Peers (future colleagues)

Do you consider this company to be an ideal employer?

Does the company support you with ongoing training and education?

How are your contributions to the organization measured?

How long have you worked for your manager?

How many hours per day do you usually work? Do you have to work weekends?

How would you characterize your boss's management style?

If you had to do it over again, would you work here?

What can you tell me about working for this company?

What do you consider the company's (department's) strengths and weaknesses?

What kind of feedback (about me) does your boss expect you to give him? How much weight has he given it in the past?

What were your expectations when you started here? Were they met? How have they changed?

Why did you decide to work here?

The hiring manager

Are there problems that keep you awake at night?

How could I make your life easier?

How would you describe the ideal candidate for this position?

If you could change one thing about the company, what would it be?

Is there anyone else along with yourself who needs to be part of this discussion so a hiring decision can be made today?

What are your own goals for this coming year? How could I specifically help you achieve them?

What have you enjoyed most about working here? Least?

What is the next step in your advancement?

What is your history with the company?

What particular traits do you value most in your subordinates?

What qualifications do you consider most essential to this position?

What's keeping you here now?

Yourself

Am I a good loser or a bad winner?

Am I a risk taker or risk averse?

Am I overly competitive? Do I give up too easily?

Am I overqualified for this position?

Am I willing to assign my copyright or patent rights to my own work to the company?

Am I willing to sign a restrictive covenant, such as a non-compete clause?

Can I do the job?

Can I live on what this company wants to pay me?

Can I achieve my ultimate career path in my current company?

Can I comfortably afford my current lifestyle?

Describe my personality.

Do I want to do the job?

Do I have the qualities generally associated with the level of responsibility/job title I am seeking?

Do I mind traveling frequently?

Do I prefer to live and work in a warm or cold climate?

Do I rise to a challenge or avoid conflict?

Does this job fit in with my long-range plans?

How can I make myself more marketable in today's competitive job market?

How can I transfer skills I already have to a completely different career?

How do my positive attributes match up with the qualities I believe are necessary for success in the job/career path I've chosen?

How does my current job differ from my ideal job?

How does my self-description match that of the culture at the company I'm considering?

How many of my positive qualities do I want to use in my job?

How many people would I ideally like to manage?

How much time am I willing to devote to a daily commute?

How well do I interact with authority figures?

How would I describe my dream job?

If I had to spend 40 hours a week doing a single activity, what would it be?

If I were to ask a group of friends and acquaintances to describe me, what adjectives would they use?

In what size city do I want to work?

In what size company do I want to work?

Is a formal employee-training program important to me?

Is a tuition reimbursement plan important to me?

What activities do I least like doing?

What activities do I most like doing?

What additional education or training would I need to achieve my dream job?

What are my goals and aspirations?

What are my key values?

What are my long-term goals?

What are my major professional accomplishments?

What are my most notable professional failures? What did I learn from them?

What are my passions?

What are my short-term goals?

Why are my strengths?

What benefits and/or perks do I require?

What can I learn from past bosses?

What competencies are my strongest calling cards?

What games and sports do I enjoy?

What has caused me to break up friendships?

What have I already done to accomplish my short-term goals?

What in my personal life causes me the most stress?

What in my personal life gives me the most pleasure?

What is important to me?

What's the lowest salary I will accept?

What is my current standard of living, and am I happy with it?

What kinds of people do I dislike working with?

What kinds of friends do I tend to have?

What kinds of people do I enjoy spending time with?

What kinds of people do I like working with?

What kinds of products/services/accounts would I prefer to work with?

What salary would I like to receive?

What specific things do I require in the job I'm seeking?

What standard of living do I aspire to in two years? Five? Ten?

What were my favorite subjects in school? Which were my strongest? Which were my weakest?

What would it take to transform myself into someone who's passionate about every workday?

What would my coworkers say about me?

What would my last boss say about my work ethic?

What would my subordinates say about me?

Where (geographically) do I want to work?

Will I fit in with this company's culture?

Who am I?

Index